# INFERNO

*Dante Alighieri*

SPARK PUBLISHING

122 Fifth Avenue
New York, NY 10011
www.sparknotes.com

ISBN 978-1-4114-6969-3

Please submit changes or report errors to www.sparknotes.com/errors.

Printed in Canada

10 9 8 7 6 5 4 3 2

# CONTENTS

# Context

ANTE ALIGHIERI WAS BORN IN 1265 IN FLORENCE, Italy, to a family of moderate wealth that had a history of involvement in the complex Florentine political scene. Around 1285, Dante married a woman chosen for him by his family, although he remained in love with another woman—Beatrice, whose true historical identity remains a mystery—and continued to yearn for her after her sudden death in 1290. Three years later, he published *Vita Nuova (The New Life)*, which describes his tragic love for Beatrice.

Around the time of Beatrice's death, Dante began a serious study of philosophy and intensified his political involvement in Florence. He held a number of significant public offices at a time of great political unrest in Italy, and, in 1302, he was exiled for life by the leaders of the Black Guelphs, the political faction in power at the time. All of Dante's work on *The Comedy* (later called *The Divine Comedy*, and consisting of three books: *Inferno, Purgatorio,* and *Paradiso*) was done after his exile. He completed *Inferno,* which depicts an allegorical journey through Hell, around 1314. Dante roamed from court to court in Italy, writing and occasionally lecturing, until his death from a sudden illness in 1321.

Dante's personal life and the writing of *The Comedy* were greatly influenced by the politics of late-thirteenth-century Florence. The struggle for power in Florence was a reflection of a crisis that affected all of Italy, and, in fact, most of Europe, from the twelfth century to the fourteenth century—the struggle between church and state for temporal authority. The main representative of the church was the pope, while the main representative of the state was the Holy Roman Emperor. In Florence, these two loyalties were represented by the Guelph party, which supported the papacy, and the Ghibelline party, which supported imperial power. The last truly powerful Holy Roman Emperor, Frederick II, died in 1250, and by Dante's time, the Guelphs were in power in Florence. By 1290, however, the Guelphs had divided into two factions: the Whites (Dante's party), who supported the independence of Florence from strict papal control, and the Blacks, who were willing to work with the pope in order to restore their power. Under the direction of Pope Boniface VIII, the Blacks gained control of Florence in 1301. Dante, as a visible and influential leader of the Whites, was exiled within a year. Dante became something of a party unto himself after his exile. His attitudes were, at times, closer to those of a Ghibelline than a Guelph, so much did he dislike Boniface. The pope, as well as a multitude of other characters from Florentine politics, has a place in the Hell that Dante depicts in *Inferno*—and not a pleasant one.

Despite the important historical context of the work, *Inferno* is far from merely a political allegory. Inferno is, for one, the exercise of an astounding intellect that handled writers such as Aristotle, Ovid, Virgil, and Thomas Aquinas with ease and skill. *Inferno* is also a landmark in the development of European language and literature, for it stands as the greatest medieval poem written in vernacular language—the common tongue of a people. Critics spanning nearly seven centuries have praised its poetic beauty and compass, virtually unmatched by any other medieval poem. Additionally, medieval Italy was home to scores of regional dialects; Dante's use of his native Tuscan dialect in *The Comedy* helped to unify the Italian language, which is rooted in Tuscan more than in any other Italian dialect. Before Dante, major literary works were almost always written in Latin, the language of the Roman Empire and the Catholic Church; no one had considered the vernacular capable of poetic expression of the caliber of Virgil's *Aeneid,* for example. Dante acknowledges the seeming folly of such an attempt by entitling his masterpiece *The Comedy* (the adjective *Divine,* indicating the religious nature of the work, was added in the sixteenth century). Obviously, Dante's choice to call his work a comedy does not mean that the poem is intended to be humorous. Rather, the word *comedy* refers to one of the two classical styles, the other being tragedy. Tragedy was the high style, the style of epics, with plots that flowed from a promising beginning to a destructive end. Comedy was the low style, the style of grotesque caricatures, with plots that flowed from an unhappy beginning to a happy end.

The title *The Comedy* is thus appropriate in two ways. First, the poem is written in the vernacular, which was considered appropriate only for a comedy. Second, the plot mirrors the flow of a classical comedy, progressing from the horrors of Hell to the joys of Heaven. Despite his seeming modesty, however, Dante was confident both that his poetry surpassed that of any other vernacular writer and that he could use the high, tragic style to perfection, as he had proved in *Vita Nuova. The Comedy* is not exclusively "high" or "low"; rather, it is a truly universal work. It deals with one of the great questions of humanity: the existence of an afterlife and the consequences of our lives on Earth. For Dante, this question was worthy of calling upon philosophers and poets alike, and of utilizing every available style, as he does throughout *Inferno*.

# PLOT OVERVIEW

INFERNO opens on the evening of Good Friday in the year 1300. Traveling through a dark wood, Dante Alighieri has lost his path and now wanders fearfully through the forest. The sun shines down on a mountain above him, and he attempts to climb up to it but finds his way blocked by three beasts—a leopard, a lion, and a she-wolf. Frightened and helpless, Dante returns to the dark wood. Here he encounters the ghost of Virgil, the great Roman poet, who has come to guide Dante back to his path, to the top of the mountain. Virgil says that their path will take them through Hell and that they will eventually reach Heaven, where Dante's beloved Beatrice awaits. He adds that it was Beatrice, along with two other holy women, who, seeing Dante lost in the wood, sent Virgil to guide him.

Virgil leads Dante through the gates of Hell, marked by the haunting inscription "ABANDON ALL HOPE, YOU WHO ENTER HERE" (III.7). They enter the outlying region of Hell, the Ante-Inferno, where the souls who in life could not commit to either good or evil now must run in a futile chase after a blank banner, day after day, while hornets bite them and worms lap their blood. Dante witnesses their suffering with repugnance and pity. The ferryman Charon then takes him and his guide across the river Acheron, the real border of Hell. The First Circle of Hell, Limbo, houses pagans, including Virgil and many of the other great writers and poets of antiquity, who died without knowing of Christ. After meeting Horace, Ovid, and Lucan, Dante continues into the Second Circle of Hell, reserved for the sin of Lust. At the border of the Second Circle, the monster Minos lurks, assigning condemned souls to their punishments. He curls his tail around himself a certain number of times, indicating the number of the circle to which the soul must go. Inside the Second Circle, Dante watches as the souls of the Lustful swirl about in a terrible storm; Dante meets Francesca, who tells him the story of her doomed love affair with Paolo da Rimini, her husband's brother; the relationship has landed both in Hell.

In the Third Circle of Hell, the Gluttonous must lie in mud and endure a rain of filth and excrement. In the Fourth Circle, the Avaricious and the Prodigal are made to charge at one another with giant boulders. The Fifth Circle of Hell contains the river Styx, a swampy, fetid cesspool in which the Wrathful spend eternity struggling with one another; the Sullen lie bound beneath the Styx's waters, choking on the mud. Dante glimpses Filippo Argenti, a former political enemy of his, and watches in delight as other souls tear the man to pieces.

Virgil and Dante next proceed to the walls of the city of Dis, a city contained within the larger region of Hell. The demons who guard the gates refuse to open them for Virgil, and an angelic messenger arrives from Heaven to force the gates open before Dante. The Sixth Circle of Hell houses the Heretics, and there Dante encounters a rival political leader named Farinata. A deep valley leads into the First Ring of the Seventh Circle of Hell, where those who were violent toward others spend eternity in a river of boiling blood. Virgil and Dante meet a group of Centaurs, creatures who are half man, half horse. One of them, Nessus, takes them into the Second Ring of the Seventh Circle of Hell, where they encounter those who were violent toward themselves (the Suicides). These souls must endure eternity in the form of trees. Dante there speaks with Pier della Vigna. Going deeper into the Seventh Circle of Hell, the travelers find those who were violent toward God (the Blasphemers); Dante meets his old patron, Brunetto Latini, walking among the souls of those who were violent toward Nature (the Sodomites) on a desert of burning sand. They also encounter the Usurers, those who were violent toward Art.

The monster Geryon transports Virgil and Dante across a great abyss to the Eighth Circle of Hell, known as Malebolge, or "evil pockets" (or "pouches"); the term refers to the circle's division into various pockets separated by great folds of earth. In the First Pouch, the Panderers and the Seducers receive lashings from whips; in the second, the Flatterers must lie in a river of human feces. The Simoniacs in the Third Pouch hang upside down in baptismal fonts while their feet burn with fire. In the Fourth Pouch are the Astrologists or Diviners, forced to walk with their heads on backward, a sight that moves Dante to great pity. In the Fifth Pouch, the Barrators (those who accepted bribes) steep in pitch while demons tear them apart. The Hypocrites in the Sixth Pouch must forever walk in circles, wearing heavy robes made of lead. Caiphas, the priest who confirmed Jesus' death sentence, lies crucified on the ground; the other sinners tread on him as they walk. In the horrifying Seventh Pouch, the Thieves sit trapped in a pit of vipers, becoming vipers themselves when bitten; to regain their form, they must bite another thief in turn.

In the Eighth Pouch of the Eighth Circle of Hell, Dante speaks to Ulysses, the great hero of Homer's epics, now doomed to an eternity among those guilty of Spiritual Theft (the False Counselors) for his role in executing the ruse of the Trojan Horse. In the Ninth Pouch, the souls of Sowers of Scandal and Schism walk in a circle, constantly afflicted by wounds that open and close repeatedly. In the Tenth Pouch, the Falsifiers suffer from horrible plagues and diseases.

Virgil and Dante proceed to the Ninth Circle of Hell through the Giants' Well, which leads to a massive drop to Cocytus, a great frozen lake. The giant Antaeus picks Virgil and Dante up and sets them down at the bottom of the well, in the lowest region of Hell. In Caina, the First Ring of the Ninth Circle of Hell, those who betrayed their kin stand frozen up to their necks in the lake's ice. In Antenora, the Second Ring, those who betrayed their country and party stand frozen up to their heads; here Dante meets Count Ugolino, who spends eternity gnawing on the head of the man who imprisoned him in life. In Ptolomea, the Third Ring, those who betrayed their guests spend eternity lying on their backs in the frozen lake, their tears making blocks of ice over their eyes. Dante next follows Virgil into Judecca, the Fourth Ring of the Ninth Circle of Hell and the lowest depth. Here, those who betrayed their benefactors spend eternity in complete icy submersion.

A huge, mist-shrouded form lurks ahead, and Dante approaches it. It is the three-headed giant Lucifer, plunged waist-deep into the ice. His body pierces the center of the Earth, where he fell when God hurled him down from Heaven. Each of Lucifer's mouths chews one of history's three greatest sinners: Judas, the betrayer of Christ, and Cassius and Brutus, the betrayers of Julius Caesar. Virgil leads Dante on a climb down Lucifer's massive form, holding on to his frozen tufts of hair. Eventually, the poets reach the Lethe, the river of forgetfulness, and travel from there out of Hell and back onto Earth. They emerge from Hell on Easter morning, just before sunrise.

# CHARACTER LIST

*Dante*  The author and protagonist of *Inferno;* the focus of all action and interaction with other characters. Because Dante chose to present his fictional poem as a record of events that actually happened to him, a wide gulf between Dante the poet and Dante the character pervades the poem. For instance, Dante the poet often portrays Dante the character as compassionate and sympathetic at the sight of suffering sinners, but Dante the poet chose to place them in Hell and devised their suffering. As a result, if Dante the character is at all representative of Dante the poet, he is a very simplified version: sympathetic, somewhat fearful of danger, and confused both morally and intellectually by his experience in Hell. As the poem progresses, Dante the character gradually learns to abandon his sympathy and adopt a more pitiless attitude toward the punishment of sinners, which he views as merely a reflection of divine justice.

*Virgil*  Dante's guide through the depths of Hell. Historically, Virgil lived in the first century B.C., in what is now northern Italy. Scholars consider him the greatest of the Latin poets. His masterpiece, the *Aeneid,* tells the story of how Aeneas, along with fellow survivors of the defeat of Troy, came to found Rome. The shade (or spirit) of Virgil that appears in *Inferno* has been condemned to an eternity in Hell because he lived prior to Christ's appearance on Earth (and thus prior to the possibility of redemption in Him). Nonetheless, Virgil has now received orders to lead Dante through Hell on his spiritual journey. Virgil proves a wise, resourceful, and commanding presence, but he often seems helpless to protect Dante from the true dangers of Hell. Critics generally consider Virgil an allegorical representation of human reason—both in its immense power and in its inferiority to faith in God.

*Beatrice*    One of the blessed in Heaven, Beatrice aids Dante's journey by asking an angel to find Virgil and bid him guide Dante through Hell. Like Dante and Virgil, Beatrice corresponds to a historical personage. Although the details of her life remain uncertain, we know that Dante fell passionately in love with her as a young man and never fell out of it. She has a limited role in *Inferno* but becomes more prominent in *Purgatorio* and *Paradiso*. In fact, Dante's entire imaginary journey throughout the afterlife aims, in part, to find Beatrice, whom he has lost on Earth because of her early death. Critics generally view Beatrice as an allegorical representation of spiritual love.

*Charon*    A figure that Dante appropriates from Greek mythology, Charon is an old man who ferries souls across the river Acheron to Hell.

*Paolo and Francesca da Rimini*   A pair of lovers condemned to the Second Circle of Hell for an adulterous love affair that they began after reading the story of Lancelot and Guinevere.

*Lucifer*    The prince of Hell, also referred to as Dis. Lucifer resides at the bottom of the Ninth (and final) Circle of Hell, beneath the Earth's surface, with his body jutting through the planet's center. An enormous giant, he has three faces but does not speak; his three mouths are busy chewing three of history's greatest traitors: Judas, the betrayer of Christ, and Cassius and Brutus, the betrayers of Julius Caesar.

*Minos*    The king of Crete in Greek mythology, Minos is portrayed by Dante as a giant beast who stands at the Second Circle of Hell, deciding where the souls of sinners shall be sent for torment. Upon hearing a given sinner's confession, Minos curls his tail around himself a specific number of times to represent the circle of Hell to which the soul should be consigned.

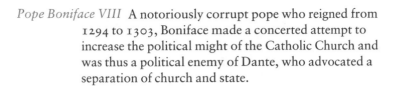

*Pope Boniface VIII*   A notoriously corrupt pope who reigned from 1294 to 1303, Boniface made a concerted attempt to increase the political might of the Catholic Church and was thus a political enemy of Dante, who advocated a separation of church and state.

*Farinata*   A Ghibelline political leader from Dante's era who resides among the Heretics in the Sixth Circle of Hell. Farinata is doomed to continue his intense obsession with Florentine politics, which he is now helpless to affect.

*Phlegyas*   The boatman who rows Dante and Virgil across the river Styx.

*Filippo Argenti*   A Black Guelph, a political enemy of Dante who is now in the Fifth Circle of Hell. Argenti resides among the Wrathful in the river Styx.

*Nessus*   The Centaur (half man and half horse) who carries Dante through the First Ring of the Seventh Circle of Hell.

*Pier della Vigna*   A former advisor to Emperor Frederick II, della Vigna committed suicide when he fell into disfavor at the court. He now must spend eternity in the form of a tree.

*Geryon*   The massive serpentine monster that transports Dante and Virgil from the Seventh to the Eighth Circle of Hell.

*Malacoda*   The leader of the Malabranche, the demons who guard the Fifth Pouch of the Eighth Circle of Hell. Malacoda (his name means "evil tail") intentionally furnishes Virgil and Dante with erroneous directions.

*Vanni Fucci*   A thief punished in the Seventh Pouch of the Eighth Circle of Hell who prophesies the defeat of the White Guelphs. A defiant soul, Fucci curses God and aims an obscene gesture at Him before Dante journeys on.

*Ulysses*  The great hero of the Homeric epics the *Iliad* and the *Odyssey*. Ulysses was a bold and cunning man who is now imprisoned in the Eighth Pouch of the Eighth Circle of Hell among those guilty of Spiritual Theft.

*Guido da Montefeltro*  An advisor to Pope Boniface VIII, da Montefeltro was promised anticipatory absolution—forgiveness for a sin given prior to the perpetration of the sin itself. Da Montefeltro now suffers in Hell, since absolution cannot be gained without repentance and it is impossible to repent a sin before committing it.

*Antaeus*  The giant who transports Dante and Virgil from the Eighth to the Ninth Circle of Hell.

*Count Ugolino*  A traitor condemned to the Second Ring of the Ninth Circle of Hell. Ugolino gnaws on the head of another damned traitor, Archbishop Ruggieri. When Ruggieri imprisoned Ugolino and his sons, denying them food, Ugolino was driven to eat the corpses of his starved sons.

*Fra Alberigo and Branca d'Oria*  Sinners condemned to the Third Ring of the Ninth Circle of Hell. Fra Alberigo and Branca d'Oria are unlike the other sinners Dante encounters: their crimes were deemed to be so great that devils snatched their souls from their living bodies; thus, their souls reside in Hell while their bodies live on, now guided and possessed by demons.

# ANALYSIS OF MAJOR CHARACTERS

## DANTE ALIGHIERI

Thirty-five years old at the beginning of the story, Dante—the character as opposed to the poet—has lost his way on the "true path" of life; in other words, sin has obstructed his path to God. *The Divine Comedy* is the allegorical record of Dante's quest to overcome sin and find God's love; in *Inferno,* Dante explores the nature of sin by traveling through Hell, where evil receives punishment according to God's justice. Allegorically, Dante's story represents not only his own life but also what Dante the poet perceived to be the universal Christian quest for God. As a result, Dante the character is rooted in the Everyman allegorical tradition: Dante's situation is meant to represent that of the whole human race.

For this reason, Dante the character does not emerge as a particularly well-defined individual; although we know that he has committed a never-specified sin and that he participates in Florentine politics, we learn little about his life on Earth. His traits are very broad and universal: often sympathetic toward others, he nonetheless remains capable of anger; he weeps at the sight of the suffering souls but reacts with pleasure when one of his political enemies is torn to pieces. He demonstrates excessive pride but remains unsatisfied in many respects: he feels that he ranks among the great poets that he meets in Limbo but deeply desires to find Beatrice, the woman he loves, and the love of God. Dante fears danger but shows much courage: horrified by Hell, he nevertheless follows his guide, Virgil, through its gates. He also proves extremely emotional, as shown by his frequent fainting when he becomes overly frightened or moved. As the story progresses, Dante must learn to reconcile his sympathy for suffering with the harsh violence of God's justice; the deeper he proceeds into Hell, the less the agonies of the damned affect him. Virgil encourages him to abhor sin and not pity the justice meted out to sinners; Dante must achieve this level of stringent moral standards before he may begin his journey to Heaven, played out in *Purgatorio* and *Paradiso.*

Because Dante the character is a fictional creation of Dante the poet, the reader should remember that the character's feelings do not always correspond to those of the poet. For instance, when Dante sees Brunetto Latini among the Sodomites in Canto XV, Dante the *character* feels deeply moved and treats his patron kindly and with compassion. But outside the poem, Dante the *poet* has chosen to condemn his former patron to damnation; by placing him among the Sodomites, he implies that Latini was homosexual, a vicious slur in fourteenth-century Italy. Indeed, on a general level, the kindness and compassion of Dante the character often contrasts with the feelings of Dante the poet, who, after all, has devised excruciating torments with which to punish his characters, many of whom are historical individuals with whom Dante was acquainted in life.

## Virgil

The only character besides Dante to appear all the way through *Inferno*, Virgil's ghost is generally taken by critics to represent human reason, which guides and protects the individual (represented by Dante/Everyman) through the world of sin. As befits a character who symbolizes reason, Virgil proves sober, measured, resolute, and wise. He repeatedly protects Dante from hostile demons and monsters, from Charon to the Centaurs; when he appears powerless outside the gates of the city of Dis in Canto VIII, his helplessness appears very ominous, signifying that Lower Hell offers far darker dangers than Upper Hell. Virgil's reliance on the angelic messenger in this scene also symbolizes the fact that reason is powerless without faith—an important tenet of Dante's moral philosophy and one that marks *Inferno* as a Christian poem, distinct from the classical epics that preceded it. In the fullest sense of the word, Virgil acts as Dante's guide, showing him not only the physical route through Hell but also reinforcing its moral lessons. When Dante appears slow to learn these lessons—such as when he sympathizes with sinners or attempts to remain too long in one region of Hell—Virgil often grows impatient with him, a trait that humanizes this otherwise impersonal shade.

Dante the character and Dante the poet seem to regard Virgil differently. Dante the character regards Virgil as his master, constantly swearing his admiration for, and trust in, him. Dante the poet, however, often makes use of *Inferno* to prove his own poetic greatness in comparison to the classical bards who preceded him—including

Virgil, who lived more than a thousand years before Dante. In Dante's time, Virgil, the author of the *Aeneid,* was considered the greatest of the Roman poets. As with many of his other classical and mythological appropriations, Dante's inclusion of Virgil in his poem denotes both an acknowledgment and appreciation of classical tradition and, to some degree, a form of bragging on Dante's part: for while he respects Virgil enough to include him in his work, he also suggests that his poem subsumes Virgil entirely.

CHARACTER ANALYSIS

# Themes, Motifs & Symbols

## Themes

*Themes are the fundamental and often universal ideas explored in a literary work.*

### The Perfection of God's Justice

Dante creates an imaginative correspondence between a soul's sin on Earth and the punishment he or she receives in Hell. The Sullen choke on mud, the Wrathful attack one another, the Gluttonous are forced to eat excrement, and so on. This simple idea provides many of *Inferno*'s moments of spectacular imagery and symbolic power, but also serves to illuminate one of Dante's major themes: the perfection of God's justice. The inscription over the gates of Hell in Canto III explicitly states that God was moved to create Hell by Justice (III.7). Hell exists to punish sin, and the suitability of Hell's specific punishments testify to the divine perfection that all sin violates.

This notion of the suitability of God's punishments figures significantly in Dante's larger moral messages and structures Dante's Hell. To modern readers, the torments Dante and Virgil behold may seem shockingly harsh: homosexuals must endure an eternity of walking on hot sand; those who charge interest on loans sit beneath a rain of fire. However, when we view the poem as a whole, it becomes clear that the guiding principle of these punishments is one of balance. Sinners suffer punishment to a degree befitting the gravity of their sin, in a manner matching that sin's nature. The design of the poem serves to reinforce this correspondence: in its plot it progresses from minor sins to major ones (a matter of degree); and in the geographical structure it posits, the various regions of Hell correspond to types of sin (a matter of kind). Because this notion of balance informs all of God's chosen punishments, His justice emerges as rigidly objective, mechanical, and impersonal; there are no extenuating circumstances in Hell, and punishment becomes a matter of nearly scientific formula.

17

Early in *Inferno*, Dante builds a great deal of tension between the objective impersonality of God's justice and the character Dante's human sympathy for the souls that he sees around him. As the story progresses, however, the character becomes less and less inclined toward pity, and repeated comments by Virgil encourage this development. Thus, the text asserts the infinite wisdom of divine justice: sinners receive punishment in perfect proportion to their sin; to pity their suffering is to demonstrate a lack of understanding.

### EVIL AS THE CONTRADICTION OF GOD'S WILL

In many ways, Dante's *Inferno* can be seen as a kind of imaginative taxonomy of human evil, the various types of which Dante classifies, isolates, explores, and judges. At times we may question its organizing principle, wondering why, for example, a sin punished in the Eighth Circle of Hell, such as accepting a bribe, should be considered worse than a sin punished in the Sixth Circle of Hell, such as murder. To understand this organization, one must realize that Dante's narration follows strict doctrinal Christian values. His moral system prioritizes not human happiness or harmony on Earth but rather God's will in Heaven. Dante thus considers violence less evil than fraud: of these two sins, fraud constitutes the greater opposition to God's will. God wills that we treat each other with the love he extends to us as individuals; while violence acts against this love, fraud constitutes a perversion of it. A fraudulent person affects care and love while perpetrating sin against it. Yet, while *Inferno* implies these moral arguments, it generally engages in little discussion of them. In the end, it declares that evil is evil simply because it contradicts God's will, and God's will does not need further justification. Dante's exploration of evil probes neither the causes of evil, nor the psychology of evil, nor the earthly consequences of bad behavior. Inferno is not a philosophical text; its intention is not to think critically about evil but rather to teach and reinforce the relevant Christian doctrines.

### STORYTELLING AS A WAY TO ACHIEVE IMMORTALITY

Dante places much emphasis in his poem on the notion of immortality through storytelling, everlasting life through legend and literary legacy. Several shades ask the character Dante to recall their names and stories on Earth upon his return. They hope, perhaps, that the retelling of their stories will allow them to live in people's memories. The character Dante does not always oblige; for example, he ignores the request of the Italian souls in the Ninth Pouch of the

Eighth Circle of Hell that he bring word of them back to certain men on Earth as warnings. However, the poet Dante seems to have his own agenda, for his poem takes the recounting of their stories as a central part of its project. Although the poet repeatedly emphasizes the perfection of divine justice and the suitability of the sinners' punishments, by incorporating the sinners' narratives into his text he also allows them to live on in some capacity aboveground.

Yet, in retelling the sinners' stories, the poet Dante may be acting less in consideration of the sinners' immortality than of his own. Indeed, Dante frequently takes opportunities to advance his own glory. Thus, for example, in Canto XXIV, halfway through his description of the Thieves' punishment, Dante declares outright that he has outdone both Ovid and Lucan in his ability to write scenes of metamorphosis and transformation (Ovid's *Metamorphoses* focuses entirely on transformations; Lucan wrote the *Pharsalia,* an account of the Roman political transition and turmoil in the first century B.C.). By claiming to have surpassed two of the classical poets most renowned for their mythological inventions and vivid imagery, Dante seeks to secure his own immortality.

Thus, Dante presents storytelling as a vehicle for multiple legacies: that of the story's subject as well as that of the storyteller. While the plot of a story may preserve the living memory of its protagonist, the story's style and skill may serve the greater glory of its author. Although many of his sinners die a thousand deaths—being burned, torn to bits, or chewed to pieces, only to be reconstituted again and again—Dante emphasizes with almost equal incessancy the power of his narrative to give both its subjects and its author the gift of eternal life.

## Motifs

*Motifs are recurring structures, contrasts, and literary devices that can help to develop and inform the text's major themes.*

### Political Arguments

An unquestionably significant part of Dante's aim in writing *Inferno* was to offer a large-scale commentary on the political nightmare of fourteenth-century Florence, from which he had recently been exiled. He makes his assertions in various ways. First, he condemns political figures with whom he disagreed by scattering them ruthlessly throughout Hell. Second, because Dante sets the action of Inferno several years before the years in which he wrote it, he can predict, as it were, certain events that had already taken place by the time of his writing. He issues these seeming predictions via the voices of the damned, apparently endowed at death with prophetic powers. In these souls' emphasis on the corruption and turmoil of the so-called future Florence, Dante aims pointed criticism at his former home. Third, Dante asserts throughout the poem his personal political belief that church and state should exist as separate but equal powers on Earth, with the former governing man's spirit and the latter governing his person. Thus, in his many references to Rome, Dante carefully mentions both its spiritual and secular importance.

The poem's arresting final image provides another testament to the equal importance of church and state: Lucifer chews both on Judas (the betrayer of Christ, the ultimate spiritual leader) and on Cassius and Brutus (the betrayers of Caesar, the ultimate political leader). Treachery against religion and against government both warrant placement in Hell's final circle. While Dante emphasizes the equality of these two institutions, he also asserts the necessity of their separation. He assigns particularly harsh punishments to souls guilty of broaching this separation, such as priests or popes who accepted bribes or yearned for political power.

### Classical Literature and Mythology

Although the values that *Inferno* asserts are decidedly Christian, on a thematic and literary level, the poem owes almost as much to Greek and Roman tradition as it does to Christian morality literature. Dante's Christian Hell features a large variety of mythological and ancient literary creatures, ranging from the Centaurs to Minos to Ulysses. He even incorporates mythological places, such as the rivers Acheron and Styx. In addition, Dante often refers to and imitates the styles of great classical writers such as Homer, Ovid, Lucan, and Virgil himself. He therefore attempts to situate himself within the tradition of classical epics while proving that he is a greater writer than any of the classical poets.

Dante incorporates this ancient material for other reasons too, including the simple fact that mythological elements contain much dramatic potential. More important, however, Dante includes mythological and classical literary elements in his poem to indicate that Christianity has subsumed these famous stories; by bringing many religious strands under one umbrella, Dante heightens the urgency and importance of his quest—a quest that he believes necessary for all human beings.

# SYMBOLS

*Symbols are objects, characters, figures, and colors used to represent abstract ideas or concepts.*

It is impossible to reduce the iconic complexity of *Inferno* to a short list of important symbols. Because the poem is an overarching allegory, it explores its themes using dozens, even hundreds, of symbols, ranging from the minutely particular (the blank banner chased by the Uncommitted in Canto III, symbolizing the meaninglessness of their activity in life) to the hugely general (the entire story of *The Divine Comedy* itself, symbolizing the spiritual quest of human life). Many of the symbols in *Inferno* are clear and easily interpretable, such as the beast Geryon—with the head of an innocent man and the body of a foul serpent, he represents dishonesty and fraud. Others are much more nuanced and difficult to pin down, such as the trio of creatures that stops Dante from climbing the sunlit mountain in Canto I. When reading *Inferno,* it is extremely important to consider each element of the poem according to how it fits into Dante's larger system of symbolism—what it says about the scene, story, and themes of the work and about human life.

Perhaps the most important local uses of symbolism in *Inferno* involve the punishments of the sinners, which are always constructed so as to correspond allegorically to the sins that they committed in life. The Lustful, for example, who were blown about by passion in life, are now doomed to be blown about by a ferocious storm for all of time. Other major types of symbols include figures who represent human qualities, such as Virgil, representative of reason, and Beatrice, representative of spiritual love; settings that represent emotional states, such as the dark forest in Canto I, embodying Dante's confusion and fear; and figures among the damned who may represent something more than merely their sins, such as Farinata, who seems to represent qualities of leadership and political commitment that transcend his identity as a Heretic in Hell.

# SUMMARY & ANALYSIS

## CANTOS I–II

### SUMMARY: CANTO I

> *Midway on our life's journey, I found myself*
> *In dark woods, the right road lost.*
> *(See* QUOTATIONS, *p. 69)*

Halfway through his life, the poet Dante finds himself wandering alone in a dark forest, having lost his way on the "true path" (I.10). He says that he does not remember how he lost his way, but he has wandered into a fearful place, a dark and tangled valley. Above, he sees a great hill that seems to offer protection from the shadowed glen. The sun shines down from this hilltop, and Dante attempts to climb toward the light. As he climbs, however, he encounters three angry beasts in succession—a leopard, a lion, and a she-wolf—which force him to turn back.

Returning in despair to the dark valley, Dante sees a human form in the woods, which soon reveals itself to be the spirit, or shade, of the great Roman poet Virgil. Thrilled to meet the poet that he most admires, Dante tells Virgil about the beasts that blocked his path. Virgil replies that the she-wolf kills all who approach her but that, someday, a magnificent hound will come to chase the she-wolf back to Hell, where she originated. He adds that the she-wolf's presence necessitates the use of a different path to ascend the hill; he offers to serve as Dante's guide. He warns Dante, however, that before they can climb the hill they must first pass through the place of eternal punishment (Hell) and then a place of lesser punishment (Purgatory); only then can they reach God's city (Heaven). Encouraged by Virgil's assurances, Dante sets forth with his guide.

### SUMMARY: CANTO II

Dante invokes the Muses, the ancient goddesses of art and poetry, and asks them to help him tell of his experiences.

Dante relates that as he and Virgil approach the mouth of Hell, his mind turns to the journey ahead and again he feels the grip of dread. He can recall only two men who have ever ventured into the afterlife and returned: the Apostle Paul, who visited the Third Circle of Heaven, and Aeneas, who travels through Hell in Virgil's *Aeneid*. Dante considers himself less worthy than these two and fears that he may not survive his passage through Hell.

Virgil rebukes Dante for his cowardice and then reassures him with the story of how he knew to find Dante and act as his guide. According to Virgil, a woman in Heaven took pity upon Dante when he was lost and came down to Hell (where Virgil lives) to ask Virgil to help him. This woman was Beatrice, Dante's departed love, who now has an honored place among the blessed. She had learned of Dante's plight from St. Lucia, also in Heaven, who in turn heard about the poor poet from an unnamed lady, most likely the Virgin Mary. Thus, a trio of holy women watches over Dante from above. Virgil says that Beatrice wept as she told him of Dante's misery and that he found her entreaty deeply moving.

Dante feels comforted to hear that his beloved Beatrice has gone to Heaven and cares so much for him. He praises both her and Virgil for their aid and then continues to follow Virgil toward Hell.

---

## ANALYSIS: CANTOS I–II

From a structural point of view, the first two cantos of *Inferno* function as an introduction, presenting the main dramatic situation and maneuvering Dante and Virgil to the entrance of Hell, the journey through which will constitute the main plot of the poem. In a larger sense, however, the opening cantos help to establish the relationship between *Inferno* and larger literary, political, and religious tradition, indicating their points of convergence and deviation.

*Inferno* takes the form of an allegory, a story whose literal plot deals entirely in symbols, imbuing the story with a second level of meaning implied by, but broader than, the events of the narrative. On a literal level, *The Divine Comedy* portrays Dante's adventures in the fantastic realms of Hell, Purgatory, and Heaven, but these adventures allegorically represent a broader subject: the trials of the human soul to achieve morality and find unity with God. From the opening lines, Dante makes clear the allegorical intention of his poem: "Midway on our life's journey, I found myself / In dark woods, the right road lost" (I.1–2). By writing "*our* life's journey" (emphasis added) and with his generic phrase "the right road," Dante links his own personal experience to that of all humanity. The dark woods symbolize sinful life on Earth, and the "right road" refers to the virtuous life that leads to God.

In this way, Dante links his poem to the larger tradition of medieval Christian allegory, most famously represented in English by Bunyan's *Pilgrim's Progress*. A great deal of medieval Christian allegory portrayed a character type known as Everyman, a Christian protagonist (even named "Christian" in Bunyan's work) representing all of humanity; the Everyman character undergoes trials and tribulations in his search to find the soul's true path in life. By making himself the hero of his story, Dante casts himself in the role of Everyman; more broadly, Dante literally wishes each individual to put him- or herself in the position described at the beginning of the poem, since, according to Christian doctrine, all people know some form of sin and thus wander lost in a dark wood. Similarly, the path to the blessed afterlife awaits anyone who seeks to find it.

The opening tercet (a three-line stanza) of *Inferno* also situates the poem in time. The Bible's Psalms describe a human lifespan as being "threescore and ten years," or seventy years. Because of the many close links between *The Divine Comedy* and the Bible, most critics agree that Dante would have considered man's lifespan to be seventy years; thus, "midway on our life's journey" would make Dante thirty-five, locating the events in the year 1300.

These cantos contain many passages, however, whose analysis has produced more disagreement than accord. For example, one can reasonably assume that the three beasts that menace Dante as he tries to climb the sunlit hill represent dark forces that threaten mankind, but it is difficult to define them more concretely. Early commentators on the poem often considered them to represent the sins of lust, pride, and avarice. The three beasts also have a biblical analogue in Jeremiah 5:6: "Wherefore a lion out of the forest shall slay them, and a wolf of the evenings shall spoil them, and a leopard shall watch over their cities." Much of the allegory in *Inferno* takes a political tone, referring to the situation in Italy (especially Florence) during Dante's lifetime, and to the conflict between the pope and the Holy Roman Emperor. It thus seems probable that the three beasts also carry political connotations, a theory reinforced by Virgil's prophecy about the hound that will drive the she-wolf away, which some critics have read as a symbol for a great leader who would one day unite Italy.

Virgil tells Dante that he lived in Rome during the time of Augustus, in the age of "the false gods who lied." The fact that Virgil recognizes the old Roman gods as "false" and "lying" (in other words, non-Christian) instances Dante's use of a technique called *intertemporality*—the mingling of elements from different time periods. Having entered into eternity, Virgil—like many of Dante's other characters—can now see into times other than those in which he lived. He is thus able to understand what Dante considers truthful theology. The use of intertemporality permeates much of the artistic and literary tradition of medieval times; biblical characters, for example, were almost always represented in art as wearing medieval clothing, and the "heathenism" of medieval Muslims was emphasized by portraying them as worshipping the ancient Greek god Apollo. Yet, while these forms of intertemporality often seem merely anachronistic, the technique is more aesthetically and logically satisfying within the context of Dante's poem: his characters can see beyond their time on Earth because in death they exist outside of time.

While Dante portrays Virgil as having learned truths from future generations, he presents himself as having gained knowledge from Virgil, commenting that the ancient poet taught him "the graceful style" that has brought him fame (I.67). The "graceful style" denotes the tragic style of the ancients, the style of epic poems—the *Odyssey*, the *Iliad*, the *Aeneid*. And Dante was indeed capable of commanding this high style; at the beginning of Canto II, his invocation of the Muses—the traditional way to begin a classical epic—echoes Virgil's call for the Muses' inspiration in the opening of the *Aeneid*. However, one may question the statement that it is this particular style that brought Dante fame: the poet elsewhere employs many other styles with equal skill. Dante clearly respects tradition but is not beholden to it, as is made clear by the way that he follows but also breaks from traditional uses of allegory, the trope of the Everyman, and intertemporality. As the remainder of the poem will make clear, his goal is not simply to mimic Virgil.

Indeed, Dante's awareness of the differences between himself and Virgil may have contributed to his decision to name his work *The Comedy*: rather than employing exclusively high rhetoric, it frequently employs the simple, vernacular idiom of its time; and rather than using Latin, the traditional language of a grand epic, it is written in Italian, the language of the people, and a language that Dante hoped every man could understand.

## CANTOS III–IV

### SUMMARY: CANTO III

> *[A]bandon all hope, you who enter here.*
> *(See* QUOTATIONS, *p. 70)*

Virgil leads Dante up to the Gate of Hell, upon which they read a foreboding inscription that includes the admonition "ABANDON ALL HOPE, YOU WHO ENTER HERE." As soon as they enter, Dante hears innumerable cries of torment and suffering. Virgil explains that these cries emanate from the souls of those who did not commit to either good or evil but who lived their lives without making conscious moral choices; therefore, both Heaven and Hell have denied them entry. These souls now reside in the Ante-Inferno, within Hell yet not truly part of it, where they must chase constantly after a blank banner. Flies and wasps continually bite them, and writhing worms consume the blood and tears that flow from them. The souls of the uncommitted are joined in this torment by the neutral angels—those who sided with neither God nor Satan in the war in Heaven.

Virgil leads Dante to a great river called Acheron, which marks the border of Hell. A crowd of newly dead souls waits to be taken across. A boat approaches with an old man, Charon, at its helm. Charon recognizes Dante as a living soul and tells him to keep away from the dead, but after Virgil informs him that their journey has been ordained from on high, Charon troubles them no longer. He returns to his work of ferrying the miserable souls, wailing and cursing, across the river into Hell. As he transports Virgil and Dante across, Virgil tells the frightened Dante that Charon's initial reluctance to ferry him bodes well: only damned souls cross the river. Suddenly, an earthquake shakes the plain; wind and fire rise up from the ground, and Dante, terrified, faints.

### SUMMARY: CANTO IV

A clap of thunder restores Dante to consciousness. When he wakes, feeling as though he has been asleep for a long time, he finds himself on the other side of the river, apparently having been carried off the boat by Virgil. He looks down into a deep valley that stretches in front of him: the First Circle of Hell, or Limbo. Virgil informs him that this circle, which contains the souls of those who led virtuous lives but either were born before the advent of Christianity (and thus could not properly honor God) or were never baptized. Dante asks if any souls have ever received permission to leave Limbo for Heaven, and Virgil names a number of Old Testament figures— Noah, Moses, and others. Christ granted these souls amnesty when he descended into Hell during the time between his death and resurrection (an episode commonly known as the Harrowing of Hell).

Many other notable figures, however, remain in Limbo. Virgil himself resides here, and has been given only a brief leave to guide Dante. Dante watches a group of men approach and greet Virgil as a fellow poet. Virgil introduces them as Homer, Horace, Ovid, and Lucan—the greatest poets of antiquity. They lead Dante to a great castle with seven walls, wherein he sees the souls of other great figures from the past: the philosophers Aristotle, Socrates, and Plato; Aeneas, Lavinia, and other characters from the *Aeneid;* the mathematician Euclid and the astronomer Ptolemy; and many others. Virgil guides Dante out of the castle and again off into the darkness.

------------

### Analysis: Cantos III–IV

In the first line of the inscription above the Gate of Hell in Canto III, "THROUGH ME YOU ENTER INTO THE CITY OF WOES," Hell is described as a city. This description gains support in the portrayal of Hell's architecture: it is walled and gated like a medieval city. The idea of cities figures significantly in *Inferno,* and Dante's treatment of them situates his poem both historically and theologically. Historically, large cities had begun to play an increasingly important role in European social and economic life in the high Middle Ages, particularly in Italy, where city-states such as Dante's native Florence had become important bases of social organization. Dante portrays Hell as a city in large part because, to a thinker in the early fourteenth century, any substantial human population would almost necessarily have suggested a city.

In the theological sense, however, *Inferno*'s treatment of cities belongs to the great tradition of St. Augustine's *City of God,* written in the early fifth century A.D. Augustine posited that all human cities center around love either of man ("the City of Man") or of God ("the City of God"). In the City of God, the forces of charity, kindness, and love bind people together; in the City of Man, each citizen acts only in his own self-interest and thus preys on his neighbor. In his various portrayals of Rome, Dante describes it as both the ultimate temporal power, a City of Man, and the spiritual center of Europe, a

City of God. This dichotomy corresponds to spiritual states within the individual: after the Judgment, those who have lived metaphorically in the City of God go to Heaven, while those who have lived in the City of Man go to Hell. The city of Hell in *Inferno*—whose inhabitants have died and been beset by divine justice—functions as a sort of phantasmagoric, supernatural representation of the City of Man. John Freccero has written that Dante's Hell, like Augustine's City of Man, represents the negative consequences of sinful desires, not just on a theological level but also on a social one.

The fourth line of the inscription raises another thematic issue, also highly visible throughout *Inferno*: the notion that God created Hell out of a concern for justice, a desire to see sin punished and virtue rewarded. One immediately notes that the punishments in Dante's Hell invariably fit the crime, in accordance with a grand sense of ultimate justice. In the Ante-Inferno, the sort of hellish suburb portrayed in Canto III, we receive our first taste of this justice. The souls of those who would not commit to either good or evil in life now must remain at the outermost limit of Hell—closest to Heaven geographically yet undeniably still a part of Hell. Dante's punishments very often have allegorical significance: the blank banner that the uncommitted souls chase symbolizes the meaninglessness of their activity on Earth (for moral choice is what gives action meaning); because these souls could not be made to act one way or another on Earth, hornets now sting them into action. Throughout the poem, this retributive justice reigns: like the souls of the uncommitted, many of the other souls in Hell are made to act out a grotesque parody of their failures on Earth.

While the punishments suffered by the damned may be "just," the text nevertheless emphasizes the pity and fear felt by the character Dante (as opposed to the poet himself) when witnessing them. Indeed, this tension is quite deliberate on the part of Dante the poet, who notes the frequent incompatibility of the human tendency to feel sorrow or pity with the relentlessly impersonal objectivity of divine justice. This tension begins to dissipate as the story progresses and the sins presented grow more heinous, for Dante gradually loses his sympathy for these increasingly evil sinners, firmly condemning their crimes as an inexcusable impediment to the fulfillment of God's will. But many of the most moving and powerful moments in *Inferno* come when Dante portrays the damned with human sympathy rather than divine impartiality, illustrating the extremity of the moral demands that Christianity makes on human beings, who are invariably fallible.

Through Canto III, the geography and organization of Dante's Hell generally conforms with medieval Catholic theology, particularly the views voiced by the thirteenth-century religious scholar Thomas Aquinas. As the characters descend into Limbo in Canto IV, however, Dante departs somewhat from these notions. Aquinas held that pagans who lived before Christ and led virtuous lives could have a place in Heaven. As the architect of his own imaginary Hell, however, Dante shows less sympathy, automatically damning those who failed to worship the Christian God, regardless of their virtue. The punishment that Dante creates for them is to know finally about the God of whom they were ignorant while they were alive. Dante seems to insist on administering justice to these figures despite his personal esteem for the great authors of antiquity, especially Virgil. With this display of unbiased judgment, he again emphasizes the immitigable, mechanical objectivity of morality and divine justice.

## CANTOS V–VI

### SUMMARY: CANTO V

> *This one, who now will never leave my side,*
> *Kissed my mouth, trembling. A Galeotto, that book!*

Dante and Virgil now descend into the Second Circle of Hell, smaller in size than the First Circle but greater in punishment. They see the monster Minos, who stands at the front of an endless line of sinners, assigning them to their torments. The sinners confess their sins to Minos, who then wraps his great tail around himself a certain number of times, indicating the number of the circle to which the soul must go. Like Charon, Minos recognizes Dante as a living soul and warns him not to enter; it is Virgil's word that again allows them to pass unmolested.

Dante and Virgil pass into a dark place in which torrential rains fall ceaselessly and gales of wind tear through the air. The souls of the damned in this circle swirl about in the wind, swept helplessly through the stormy air. These are the Lustful—those who committed sins of the flesh.

Dante asks Virgil to identify some of the individual souls to him; they include many of great renown, including Helen, for whose sake the Trojan War was fought, and Cleopatra. Dante immediately feels sympathy for these souls, for essentially they are damned by love. With Virgil's permission, he calls out to the souls to see if they will speak to him and tell him their story. One woman, Francesca, recognizes Dante as a living soul and answers him. She relates to him how love was her undoing: bound in marriage to an old and deformed man, she eventually fell in love with Paolo da Rimini, her husband's younger brother. One day, as she and Paolo sat reading an Arthurian legend about the love of Lancelot and Guinevere, each began to feel that the story spoke to their own secret love. When they came to a particularly romantic moment in the story, they could not resist kissing. Francesca's husband quickly discovered their transgression and had the young lovers killed. Now Paolo and Francesca are doomed to spend eternity in the Second Circle of Hell. Overcome with pity, Dante faints again.

## Summary: Canto VI

When Dante wakes, he finds that he has been moved to the Third Circle of Hell, where the rains still fall. Now, however, the drops consist of filth and excrement, and a horrific stench fills the air. A three-headed dog, Cerberus, tries to stop Virgil and Dante's progress, but Virgil satisfies the beast by throwing it a chunk of earth. Dante and Virgil then advance into the circle of the Gluttonous, who must lie on the ground as the sewage rains down upon them.

One of the Gluttonous sits up when he sees Virgil and Dante, and asks if Dante recognizes him. When Dante replies that he does not, the shade announces himself as Ciacco, saying that he spent his earthly life in Florence. At Dante's request, he voices his predictions for Florence's political future, which he anticipates will be filled with strife. Dante then asks about figures from Florence's political past, naming individuals he believes to have been well intentioned. Ciacco replies that they reside in a much deeper circle of Hell. Before lying back down, he asks Dante to remember his name when he returns to the world above.

As they leave the Third Circle, Dante asks Virgil how the punishments of the souls will change after the Last Judgment. Virgil replies that since that day will bring the perfection of all creation, their punishments will be perfected as well.

## ANALYSIS: CANTOS V–VI

Dante draws the character of Minos both from the *Aeneid* and from ancient mythology, just as he takes the three-headed dog Cerberus from Greek stories of the afterlife. By placing pagan gods and monsters in an otherwise Christian model of the afterlife, Dante once again demonstrates his tendency to mix vastly different religious and mythological traditions. This tendency speaks to two main aspects underlying the poem. First, it indicates the extent to which mythological and literary sources share space in Dante's imagination with religious and theological sources; Dante intends his work as a partly cultural and partly spiritual project. But this tendency also reflects Dante's intentions within the spiritual half of his project: he attempts to show Christianity as a supreme moral order. By subsuming pagan gods into the Christian conception of Hell, he privileges Christian thought as the authoritative system.

Like the punishments administered in the prior circles, the punishments here correspond in grotesque aptness to the sins themselves. Thus, the Lustful, those who were obsessed with the stimulation of the flesh in life, now have their nerves unceasingly stimulated by the storm. Also, they lie prone and in the dark—the conditions in which acts of lust generally take place. Finally, because they failed to restrain the internal tempests of their emotions, external tempests now bludgeon their bodies. The punishment of the Gluttonous, whose sins also involved an obsession with bodily pleasure, is similarly appropriate. Those who excessively pursued pleasure in life now lie in an overabundance of that which disgusts. The excrement that douses them constitutes both the literal and figurative product of their greedy and wasteful consumption.

Although Dante the poet remorselessly assigns illicit lovers to Hell, one senses that he may join his character Dante in pitying them their fates. Dante the poet intends to assert the existence of an objectively just moral universe; yet he also imbues Paolo and Francesca with great human feeling, and the sensual language and romantic style with which he tells their story has made this canto one of the most famous in the poem. Moreover, we know that the poet Dante's own life was marked by a deep love, his love for Beatrice, which he so beautifully expresses in his earlier poem *Vita Nuova*. Still, his damnation of the lovers suggests a moral repudiation of his own biographical and poetic past; in a certain sense, *The Divine Comedy* as a whole can be read as Dante's attempt to transpose his earthly love for Beatrice onto a spiritual, Christian, morally perfect plane. Part of this process involves renouncing earthly romance, however appealing it might seem, in favor of the saintly perfections of Heaven.

While Dante's sympathy for Paolo and Francesca remains only implicit, this sympathy translates into occasional breaks with the moral order he asserts, making Dante more lenient in the punishments he assigns. Dido, for example, was a mythological queen who committed suicide because of her unrequited love for Aeneas. Most souls that have committed suicide end up far deeper in Hell, as we see later, but Dante chooses to punish Dido in accordance only with her lesser sin—that of loving too much. Dante's favoritism emerges even more clearly later in the poem, when we witness his treatment of other souls similarly guilty of multiple sins: to these he assigns punishments in accordance with their gravest crimes.

Canto VI offers the poem's first extensive discussion of Italian politics, a subject that figures in many of its allegorical as well as its most literal passages. In this case, Dante largely discards allegory to write openly of the political situation in Florence. Because Dante wrote his poem circa 1310–1314, several years after the year in which its plot takes place (1300), he can "predict," as it were, through the mouth of Ciacco, the political events of the next few years. Ciacco's depiction of Florence as a city divided refers to the struggle for control between the Black and White Guelphs at the turn of the century. Ciacco describes a bloody fight between the two factions that occurred on May 1, 1300, and which resulted in the Whites gaining power, though only for a few years. The Blacks subsequently returned to power and exiled hundreds of Whites, including Dante, who never forgave the people of Florence for his banishment from his beloved city. He allegedly titled his work "The Comedy of Dante Alighieri, a Florentine by birth but not in character"—a clear indication of his disgust with the infighting that plagued Florence.

This canto also provides further insight into the material characteristics of Dante's Hell. As Virgil notes, the dead do not have their earthly bodies at the time of Dante's journey; in fact, the two poets physically tread upon shades as they cross the Third Circle of Hell. Virgil points out that each soul will regain its flesh at the Last Judgment. But this statement raises the question of how these souls without bodies can nonetheless suffer physical torment. We must assume that they possess *some* sort of solid form; otherwise, Dante would not be able to see them.

## CANTOS VII–IX

### SUMMARY: CANTO VII

Virgil and Dante continue down toward the Fourth Circle of Hell and come upon the demon Plutus. Virgil quiets the creature with a word and they enter the circle, where Dante cries out at what he sees: a ditch has been formed around the circle, making a great ring. Within the ring, two groups of souls push weights along in anger and pain. Each group completes a semicircle before crashing into the other group and turning around to proceed in the opposite direction. The souls condemned to this sort of torturous, eternal jousting match, Virgil explains, are those of the Avaricious and the Prodigal, who, during their lives, hoarded and squandered, respectively, their money.

Dante, as before, inquires whether he knows any of the souls here. Virgil informs him that most of the Avaricious are corrupt clergymen, popes, and cardinals but adds that the experiences they undergo here render them unrecognizable. He notes that the Avaricious and Prodigal share one essential characteristic: they were not prudent with the goods of Fortune. Dante asks Virgil to explain the nature of this "Fortune." Virgil replies that Fortune has received orders from God to transfer worldly goods between people and between nations. Her swift movements evade human understanding; thus, men should not curse her when they lose their possessions.

Pondering this explanation, Dante follows Virgil down to the Fifth Circle of Hell, which borders the muddy river Styx. They see souls crouched on the bank, covered in mud, and striking and biting at each other. They are the Wrathful, those who were consumed with anger during their lives. Virgil alerts Dante to the presence of additional souls here, which remain invisible to him as they lie completely submerged in the Styx—these are the Sullen, those who muttered and sulked under the light of the sun. They now gurgle and choke on the black mud of the swampy river.

### SUMMARY: CANTO VIII

Continuing around the Fifth Circle of Hell, Virgil and Dante come to a tall tower standing on the bank, its pinnacle bursting with flames. Virgil and Dante encounter the boatman Phlegyas, who takes them across the Styx at Virgil's prompting. On the way, they happen upon a sinner whom Dante angrily recognizes as Filippo Argenti. He has no pity for Argenti and gladly watches the other sinners tear him apart as the boat pulls away.

Virgil announces that they are now approaching the city of Dis— Lower Hell. As they near the entrance, a host of fallen angels cries out. They demand to know why one of the living dares to try to enter Dis. Virgil again provides a rationale for Dante's presence, but, for the first time, he proves unsuccessful in gaining entrance. The demons slam the gate in Virgil's face, and he returns to Dante hurt but not defeated.

## Summary: Canto IX

Dante grows pale with fear upon seeing Virgil's failure. Virgil, who appears to be waiting for someone impatiently, weakly reassures Dante. Suddenly, Dante sees three Furies—creatures that are half woman, half serpent. They shriek and laugh when they notice Dante, and call for Medusa to come and turn him into stone. Virgil quickly covers Dante's eyes so that he will not see Medusa's head.

An enormous noise from behind scatters the Furies. Virgil and Dante turn to see a messenger from Heaven approaching across the river Styx, with souls and demons fleeing before him like flies. He arrives at the gate and demands that it be opened for the travelers; he is promptly obeyed. Virgil and Dante pass through the gate of Dis and enter the Sixth Circle of Hell. Tombs surround them, glowing among fiercely hot flames; here lie the Heretics.

## Analysis: Cantos VII–IX

The symbolic correspondences between crimes and their punishments, visible here as in the other cantos, display Dante's allegorical ingenuity and contribute to his exploration of the larger theme of divine justice. Justice in *Inferno* is continually portrayed as a matter of precise, almost mechanical, dispensation, as evidenced by Minos's methodical curling of his tail, in Canto V, to assign each damned soul to its proper torment. Not only is God's justice coldly impersonal and utterly without pity, it is meted out with extremely careful balance: in each level of Hell, damned souls suffer in both kind and degree, according to the type and extremity of their sins on Earth.

The concept of God's retribution not only plays a thematically important role in *Inferno*; it also lends structure to the poem's geography, as well as to its narrative form. The geographical settings through which the characters progress correspond to *kinds* of sin— the swampy Styx for the Sullen, for example, and the tempest for the

Lustful—providing a sequence of powerful physical illustrations of Dante's abstract messages. The narrative form of *Inferno* unfolds in accordance with the *degree* of sin: the degree of evil and torment that Dante the character encounters escalates as the story progresses, enabling Dante the poet to create increasingly intense episodes. These episodes help him to make his moral points with added force, and to develop Dante the character. Their evenly spaced gradations of torment allow Dante to build psychological and emotional tension at an impeccably controlled pace.

This extraordinary correspondence between narrative, setting, and theme remains one of *Inferno*'s most remarkable aspects, and has helped to secure the work's position in the Western canon. In the scene of the Avaricious and the Prodigal in Canto VII, we see a particularly vivid instance of this correlation. Dante thematically joins these two sins by placing them within the same physical space and temporal episode. Seemingly opposite, Dante notes the similarity of these sins: both involve imprudence with money or material goods. The text's notion of the value of prudence stems from Aristotelian philosophy, to which Dante adheres throughout *The Divine Comedy* with few exceptions. Aristotle praised the virtue of moderation, or what he called the mean; in his view, one should avoid the extremes of passion and guide oneself by reason. This restraint, however, is not to be confused with the noncommittal nature of the souls in the Ante-Inferno, who avoided extremes not out of reason but out of cowardice; indeed, reason often calls for us to take sides on moral issues.

Whereas the Second through Fifth Circles of Hell contain those who could not hold fast to the Aristotelian mean, the Sixth Circle of Hell seems to be of a different type: the Heretics have committed a sin not of indulgence or excess but rather of rejection. Fittingly, the poem marks a significant geographic separation between the Fifth and Sixth Circles of Hell, which represent the border between Upper Hell and Lower Hell. Lower Hell stands apart as the city of Dis, a sort of subcity within the city of Hell. Virgil's helplessness at the gates of Dis signify that he and Dante have now entered into a new, more insidious and dangerous kind of sinfulness. Up to this point, Virgil has confidently protected Dante. As Virgil and Dante pass into Lower Hell, the sense of physical and spiritual danger to the travelers grows in proportion with the sin and suffering of the damned souls.

Dante's reaction to Filippo Argenti in these cantos marks a sudden departure from his previous pity for the damned. This shift could be seen as illuminating both Dante the poet and Dante the character. Argenti was a Black Guelph in Florence, and his brother may have taken the poet Dante's property after the latter's exile. Though Homer, Horace, Dido, and Aeneas are well known to modern audiences, they receive significantly less treatment than Argenti, with whom readers would otherwise be unfamiliar. Apparently, the poet's desire to vent his personal anger here overwhelms his desire to reference the larger culture. Perhaps more important, this scene furthers the development of Dante the character. For his departure from sympathy proves a permanent one, as he begins to grow ever more intolerant of sin and less inclined to pity the sinners' torments. Virgil condones this growing contempt, and Dante the poet seems to advocate it. He implies that, on an ultimate level, sin is unacceptable and not to be pitied. The scenes in Upper Hell witness a tension between the main character's human sympathy and the objective impersonality of God's justice; as the poem progresses, divine justice wins out.

Finally, these cantos include two notable references to beings from classical mythology; in typical fashion, Dante seamlessly incorporates these beings into a Christian Hell. Virgil describes Fortune as a minister of God and yet gives her all of the pagan characteristics that normally accompany her in ancient myth. The Furies and the legend of Medusa's head come straight from Ovid's *Metamorphoses,* one of the favorite sources of mythology for medieval writers and thinkers. The Furies seem a bit out of place here, as they do nothing to advance the plot—they simply threaten Dante before being scared off. In part, Dante uses this passage to flex his poetic muscles, as if declaring that anything worthwhile in the poetry of the ancients falls within his territory as well. Dante's deft incorporation of various traditions contributes to the creation of his own distinctive style.

## Cantos X–XI

### Summary: Canto X

Still in the Sixth Circle of Hell, Dante and Virgil wander among the fiery tombs of the Heretics. Virgil describes the particular heresy of one of the groups, the Epicureans, who pursued pleasure in life because they believed that the soul died with the body. Suddenly, a voice from one of the tombs interrupts them and addresses Dante as a Tuscan (Tuscany is the region of Italy in which Florence is located). The voice belongs to a soul whom Virgil identifies as Farinata, a political leader of Dante's era. Virgil encourages Dante to speak with him.

Dante and Farinata have hardly begun their conversation when another soul, that of Cavalcante de' Cavalcanti, the father of Dante's intimate friend Guido, rises up and interrupts them, wondering why his son has not accompanied Dante here. Dante replies that perhaps Guido held Virgil in disdain. (According to some translations of *Inferno,* Dante says that Guido held God, or Beatrice, in disdain. The point is a matter of considerable debate among scholars.) Frantic, the shade reads too much into Dante's words and assumes that his son is dead. In despair, he sinks back down in his grave.

Farinata continues discussing Florentine politics. He and Dante clearly represent opposing parties (though these parties are not named), yet they treat each other politely. From Farinata's words and those of the nearby soul, Dante realizes that the shades in Hell can see future events but not present ones. Farinata can prophesy the future—he predicts Dante's exile from Florence—but remains ignorant of current events. Farinata confirms that, as part of their punishment, the Heretics can see only distant things.

Virgil calls Dante back, and they proceed through the rest of the Sixth Circle. Farinata's words have made Dante apprehensive about the length of time remaining for his exile, but Virgil assures him that he will hear a fuller account when they come to a better place.

### SUMMARY: CANTO XI

At the edge of the Seventh Circle of Hell rises a stench so overpowering that Virgil and Dante must sit down at the tomb of Pope Anastasius in order to adjust to it. Virgil takes the opportunity to explain the last three circles of Hell and their respective subdivisions. The Seventh Circle of Hell, which contains those who are violent, is subdivided into three smaller circles: they punish the sins of violence against one's neighbor, against oneself, and against God. Worse than any violence, however, is the sin of fraud, which breaks the trust of a man and therefore most directly opposes the great virtue of love. The last two circles of Hell thus punish the Fraudulent. The Eighth Circle punishes "normal fraud"—sins that violate the natural trust between people. Such fraud includes acts of hypocrisy and underhanded flattery. The Ninth Circle, the seat of Dis, punishes betrayal—sins that violate a relationship of particularly special trust. These are the loyalties to kin, to country and party, to guests, and to benefactors.

Dante asks Virgil why these divisions of Hell exist, wondering why the sinners they have seen previously do not receive this same degree of punishment, as they too have acted contrary to divine will. In response, Virgil reminds Dante of the philosophy set forth in Aristotle's Nicomachean Ethics, which posits the existence of "[t]hree dispositions counter to Heaven's will: / Incontinence, malice, insane brutality" (XI.79–80). The disposition of incontinence offends God least, says Virgil, and thus receives a more lenient punishment, outside of the city of Dis.

Dante then asks for clarification of one more theological issue: why is usury a sin? Virgil explains to Dante that usury goes against God's will because a usurer makes his money not from industry or skill ("art")—as Genesis stipulates that human beings should—but rather from money itself (in the form of interest). Thus, usurers also go against God's "art," or His design for the world. The two poets now progress toward the First Ring of the Seventh Circle of Hell.

### ANALYSIS: CANTOS X–XI

Of all the cantos, Canto X may narrate the most action at the fastest pace; it also contains a remarkable amount of lyricism. Indeed, Dante's adroit leaps between topics and moods play an important role in creating the poetic force of the canto. Farinata interrupts Virgil and Dante without a word of prelude from Dante the poet. The sharp, seemingly transitionless movement between one speech and another had almost no precedent in vernacular literature of the time. A second interruption occurs when Cavalcanti, the other soul, breaks in. Yet this intrusion does not faze Farinata, who continues in his slow, dignified manner despite the other's anxious exclamations; Dante maintains the two distinct tones simultaneously. This scene possesses a less uniform voice than the rest of the poem; it achieves its force through its contrasts. Dante juxtaposes Farinata's piercing gaze, for instance, with the darting, anxious eyes of Cavalcanti, and implicitly compares Farinata's impassioned love for Florence and his people with Cavalcanti's poignant love for his son Guido. Dante thus brings out the intimately emotional side of political loyalty while showing the nobility in the seemingly humble love between father and son.

The conversation between Farinata and Dante also contributes to *Inferno*'s exploration of politics and history. Historically, Farinata served as a leader of the Ghibellines, the party that opposed Dante's Guelphs, and was banished from Florence with the rest of his party, never to return. By the time of Dante's writing, however, the Guelphs had split into two factions, occasioning a second set of banishments: the Black Guelphs had gained control and exiled the White Guelphs, including Dante. As a result, Dante the poet felt a connection to the Ghibellines; hence his peaceable conversation here with Farinata.

One of the most impressive aspects of *Inferno* is the imaginative power with which Dante evokes suffering and torment, the skill with which he creates a fictional Hell out of a pastiche of poetic styles and philosophical and religious ideas. These cantos, for instance, repeatedly conflate biblical and Aristotelian moral arguments. In Dante's portrayals of Farinata and Cavalcanti, we see the skill with which the poet evokes psychological suffering in particular. Theirs is a brilliant example of psychological torture; it depends entirely on the Christian conception of the man as an essentially indestructible being with an immortal soul that mirrors the personality. Dante takes this conception to a remarkable conclusion—in Hell, one cannot be different from how one was on Earth. This inability to restore oneself to God's favor is precisely what makes Hell so terrible—one can clearly see one's mistake but is doomed, even forced, to repeat it endlessly.

After the dense Canto X, Canto XI provides a welcome break in the action if not in the philosophical development. Virgil's explanation of the organization of Hell reveals its accordance with the moral order in Aristotle's *Nicomachean Ethics*. As we have already seen, Dante is indebted to Aristotle for the majority of his philosophical, if not his theological, ideas (we recall the notion of the mean). With Virgil's discussion of incontinence, malice, and insane brutality, our picture of Hell nears completion; the remaining geographical subdivisions of the poem's setting correspond to subtle differences among the sins of violence and among the sins of fraud.

## Cantos XII–XIII

### Summary: Canto XII
The passage to the First Ring of the Seventh Circle of Hell takes Virgil and Dante through a ravine of broken rock. At the edge, the

monstrous Minotaur threatens them, and they must slip past him while he rages to distraction. As they descend, Virgil notes that this rock had not yet fallen at the time of his previous journey into the depths of Hell. Coming into the ring, they see a river of blood: here boil the sinners who were violent against their neighbors. A group of Centaurs—creatures that are half man, half horse—stand on the bank of the river with bows and arrows. They shoot at any soul that tries to raise itself out of the river to a height too pleasant for the magnitude of his or her sin.

The head Centaur, Chiron, notices that Dante moves the rocks that he walks on as only a living soul would. He draws an arrow, but Virgil commands him to stand back, and he obeys. Because the broken rocks make the ring treacherous to navigate, Virgil also asks that a Centaur be provided to guide them through the ring around the boiling blood. Chiron provides one named Nessus, on whose back Dante climbs.

Leading Virgil and Dante through the ring, Nessus names some of the more notable souls punished here, including one called Alexander (probably Alexander the Great), Dionysius, and Atilla the Hun. Those who lived as tyrants, and thus perpetrated violence on whole populations, lie in the deepest parts of the river. After fording the river at a shallow stretch, Nessus leaves the travelers, who continue on into the Second Ring.

## SUMMARY: CANTO XIII

In the Second Ring of the Seventh Circle of Hell, Virgil and Dante enter a strange wood filled with black and gnarled trees. Dante hears many cries of suffering but cannot see the souls that utter them. Virgil cryptically advises him to snap a twig off of one of the trees. He does so, and the tree cries out in pain, to Dante's amazement. Blood begins to trickle down its bark. The souls in this ring—those who were violent against themselves or their possessions (Suicides and Squanderers, respectively)—have been transformed into trees.

Virgil tells the damaged tree-soul to tell his story to Dante so that Dante may spread the story on Earth. The tree-soul informs them that in life he was Pier della Vigna, an advisor to Emperor Frederick, and that he was a moral and admirable man. But when an envious group of scheming courtiers blackened his name with lies, he felt such shame that he took his own life.

Dante then asks how the souls here came to be in their current state. The tree-soul explains that when Minos first casts souls here, they take root and grow as saplings. They then are wounded and pecked by Harpies—foul creatures that are half woman, half bird. When a tree-soul's branch is broken, it causes the soul the same pain as dismemberment. When the time comes for all souls to retrieve their bodies, these souls will not reunite fully with theirs, because they discarded them willingly. Instead, the returned bodies will be hung on the soul-trees' branches, forcing each soul to see and feel constantly the human form that it rejected in life.

At this point, two young men run crashing through the wood, interrupting Dante's conversation with the tree-soul. One of the men, Jacomo da Sant'Andrea, falls behind and leaps into a bush; vicious dogs have been pursuing him, and now they rend him to pieces. Virgil and Dante then speak to the bush, which is also a soul: it speaks of the suffering that has plagued Florence ever since it decided to make St. John the Baptist its patron, replacing its old patron, Mars (a Roman god). The bush-soul adds that he was a Florentine man in life who hanged himself.

### Analysis: Cantos XII–XIII

When Virgil comments in Canto XII about the broken rocks he and Dante must navigate, he alludes to the earthquake that, according to the Gospels, occurred upon Christ's crucifixion. Noting that the rocks had not yet fallen when he first descended into Hell, in the late first century B.C., Virgil reasons that they must have broken during the abovementioned earthquake, after which Christ came down to Hell to free a number of souls, including the Old Testament prophets ("The great spoil of the upper circle" [XII.33]). Virgil thus reasons that the earthquake seen by evangelists on Earth in fact penetrated to the underworld as well. Dante implies that Christ's death shook Hell to its very roots, both literally and figuratively.

Virgil's comment also seems to suggest that Hell experiences the effects of the passage of time: Virgil can remember a physically different Hell, and the souls can anticipate the return of their bodies. This notion of Hell possessing a past, present, and future would seem to contradict the eternal nature of the place. However, Hell does not seem vulnerable to the force of time per se, but rather to the force of God's will over time. The changes in Hell mentioned here correspond to two divine events: the Harrowing and the Last Judgment. After this second event, time will disappear altogether.

The pool of boiling blood serves as an allegorically apt punishment for those who were violent toward others: they sit eternally submerged in the blood after which they lusted in life. This punishment, like so many in Dante's Hell, proves impeccably flexible according to the sinners' degrees of sin, allowing for individualized penalties of excruciating exactitude. The soul of an individual who killed only one person, for example, stands with his legs in the burning blood, while the soul of a tyrant such as Alexander stands with his entire head covered. The scene also provides Dante with an opportunity to voice his politics: while a more objective view of history might rank many other leaders among these tyrants, Dante exempts them from punishment here. The conspicuous absence of Roman leaders in particular testifies to Dante's great reverence for Rome.

It seems odd at first that the Suicides' punishment is to be turned into trees; the reader does not see how this punishment fits into Dante's usual pattern until one of the trees begins his speech about the Last Judgment. Then we see how the punishment fits the crime: having discarded their bodies on Earth, these souls are rendered unable to assume human form for the rest of eternity. In committing suicide, these souls denied their God-given immortality and declared that they did not want their bodies; their punishment is to get their wish only after they have recognized the error in it.

Finally, at the end of Canto XIII, the bush-soul gives us some interesting information about the history of Florence. When Florence was Christianized, it abandoned the god Mars as its patron and turned its allegiance toward John the Baptist. The "art" of Mars is war; his resentment at being replaced, the bush asserts, causes Florence to be plagued by infighting. Dante here employs the common classical device of using mythological legend to account for earthly events, a device found frequently in ancient Greek and Roman literature. Yet he is only half-serious about this explanation: *Inferno*'s frequent political jabs make it clear that Dante has plenty of flesh-and-blood enemies on whom to blame Florence's civil strife.

## Cantos XIV–XVII

### Summary: Canto XIV

Dante gathers the bush's scattered leaves and gives them to the bush. He and Virgil then proceed through the forest of tree-souls to the edge of the Third Ring of the Seventh Circle of Hell. Here they find a desert of red-hot sand, upon which flakes of fire drift down slowly but ceaselessly. As Virgil expounded in Canto XI, this ring, reserved for those who were violent against God, is divided into three zones.

SUMMARY & ANALYSIS

The rain of fire falls throughout all three. The First Zone is for the Blasphemers, who must lie prone on a bank of sand. The falling flakes of fire keep the sand perpetually hot, ensuring that the souls burn from above and below. Among these sinners Dante sees a giant, whom Virgil identifies as Capaneus, one of the kings who besieged Thebes. Capaneus rages relentlessly, insisting that the tortures of Hell shall never break his defiance.

The poets reach another river, which runs red, and Virgil speaks to Dante about the source of Hell's waters. Underneath a mountain on the island of Crete sits the broken statue of an Old Man. Tears flow through the cracks in the statue, gathering at his feet. As they stream away, they form the Acheron, the Styx, the Phlegethon, and finally Cocytus, the pool at the bottom of Hell.

### SUMMARY: CANTO XV

Crossing the stream, Virgil and Dante enter the Second Zone of the Seventh Circle's Third Ring, where the Sodomites—those violent against nature—must walk continuously under the rain of fire. One of these souls, Brunetto Latini, recognizes Dante and asks him to walk near the sand for a while so that they may converse. Latini predicts that Dante will be rewarded for his heroic political actions. Dante dismisses this prediction and says that Fortune will do as she pleases. Virgil approves of this attitude, and they move on as Latini returns to his appointed path.

### SUMMARY: CANTO XVI

Still in the Second Zone among the Sodomites, Dante is approached by another group of souls, three of whom claim to recognize Dante as their countryman. The flames have charred their features beyond recognition, so they tell Dante their names. Dante recalls their names from his time in Florence and feels great pity for them. They ask if courtesy and valor still characterize their city, but Dante sadly replies that acts of excess and arrogance now reign.

Before leaving the Second Zone, Virgil makes a strange request. He asks for the cord that Dante wears as a belt, then throws one end of it into a ravine filled with dark water. Dante watches incredulously as a horrible creature rises up before them.

### SUMMARY: CANTO XVII

Dante now sees that the creature has the face of a man, the body of a serpent, and two hairy paws. Approaching it, he and Virgil descend into the Third Zone of this circle's Third Ring. Virgil stays to speak with the beast, sending Dante ahead to explore the zone, inhabited by those who were violent against art (Virgil has earlier denoted them as the Usurers). Dante sees that these souls must sit beneath the rain of fire with purses around their necks; these bear the sinners' respective family emblems, which each "with hungry eyes consumed" (XVII.51). As they appear unwilling to talk, Dante returns to Virgil.

In the meantime, Virgil has talked the human-headed monster into transporting them down to the Eighth Circle of Hell. Fearful but trusting of his guide, Dante climbs onto the beast's serpentine back; Virgil addresses their mount as "Geryon." To Dante's terror and amazement, Geryon rears back and suddenly takes off into the air, circling slowly downward. After setting them down safely among the rocks at the edge of the Eighth Circle of Hell, Geryon returns to his domain.

## Analysis: Cantos XIV–XVII

Throughout *Inferno,* Dante the poet explains and clarifies the geography of his Hell in the form of periodic lectures given by Virgil to Dante the character. Canto XIV instances one such explanation. The "Old Man"—the statue from which the four rivers of Hell flow—derives in part from the poetry of Ovid and in part from the Bible's Book of Daniel. Many critics interpret the crumbling statue as representing the decline of mankind. Virgil describes it as comprising four materials: gold, silver, brass, and iron. Understood as a series, these metals correspond to the four ages of human history that Ovid delineates in his *Metamorphoses:* the Golden Age, Silver Age, Bronze (or Brass) Age, and Iron Age. The left leg of the statue, made of iron, can be seen to represent the Roman Empire, strong and willfully led, while the right leg, made of clay, could be the Catholic Church—cracked by its corruption. Additionally, the statue looks west, toward Rome, in hope of renewal. This statue, along with the beasts at the beginning of the poem and Dante's cord in Canto XVI, belongs to a group of apparently allegorical objects in *Inferno* whose symbolic meaning remains ambiguous. Dante may intend them simply to stimulate the imagination, and to add a sense of mystique to the world of his poem.

Brunetto Latini was a Florentine Guelph, renowned for both his writing and his politics; he taught at the university where Dante studied and helped foster Dante's career. Although Latini provided him in life with kindness and counsel, the poet Dante rather ungratefully places him in Hell, and implicitly accuses his teacher of homosexuality or pedophilia, situating him among the Sodomites.

Perhaps the negative treatment received by Latini at the hands of Dante testifies to a positive aspect of the poem itself. Although Dante often uses *Inferno* to make jabs at his political enemies and "reward" his allies, this scene suggests that the work transcends mere political propaganda. Thus, although he places many Black Guelphs and Ghibellines in Hell, along with a number of popes, Dante also sees the flaws among his own White Guelphs, declaring, "so long as conscience is not betrayed, / I am prepared for Fortune to do her will" (XV.89–90). Thus while he may promote particular emperors, and while he certainly doesn't repress his anger at the papists, he puts forth the following of one's conscience as the most important rule to follow, regardless of party. This attempt to shift his judgments out of partisan territory also points out religion as Dante's underlying priority: regardless of one's political beliefs, sin against God still merits full punishment.

Yet while Dante may maintain religion as the guiding force behind his work, he forgoes few opportunities to make political asides. In Canto XVI, as he talks with the three Florentine souls, Dante continues to reveal his pessimism about the political state of affairs in Florence. His description of the city reflects his state of exile—it is clearly a view from the outside. Moreover, the kinship he feels toward these souls stems from more than his sense of their common geographical origins; it comes from his sense of their common fate. For these three damned sinners are also exiles in their way. Thus, like Dante, they stand in this scene with their eyes turned back toward home, bemoaning the evil that is overrunning Florence but unable to do anything about it.

Dante draws the strange beast Geryon, the guardian of the Eighth Circle of Hell, from classical mythology, changing his form and reducing his number of heads but preserving his status as a symbol of fraud. Having left behind the circles punishing various types of violence, Virgil and Dante now enter the final two circles. While these circles contain many subdivisions of their own, they are both devoted to punishing the greatest sin of all—malice, or fraud. As a symbol of fraud, Geryon signifies this transition.

# Cantos XVIII–XX

## Summary: Canto XVIII

Virgil and Dante find themselves outside the Eighth Circle of Hell, known as Malebolge ("Evil Pouches"). Dante describes the relationship between the circle's structure and its name: the circle has a wall running along the outside and features a great circular pit at its center; ten evenly spaced ridges run between the wall and the pit. These ridges create ten separate pits, or pouches, in which the perpetrators of the various forms of "ordinary fraud" receive their punishments. Virgil leads Dante around the left side of the circle, where they come upon the First Pouch.

Here, Virgil and Dante see a group of souls running constantly from one side of the pouch to the other. On both of the pouch's containing ridges, demons with great whips scourge the souls as soon as they come within reach, forcing them back to the opposite ridge. Dante recognizes an Italian there and speaks to him; the soul informs Dante that he lived in Bologna and now dwells here because he sold his sister to a noble. This pouch is for the Panders (pimps) and the Seducers—those who deceive women for their own advantage. Moving on, Virgil and Dante also see the famous Jason of mythology, who abandoned Medea after she helped him find the Golden Fleece.

As Virgil and Dante cross the ridge to the Second Pouch, a horrible stench besieges them, and they hear mournful cries. Dante beholds a ditch full of human excrement, into which many sinners have been plunged. From one of these souls, he learns that this pouch contains the Flatterers. After a few seconds, Virgil says that they have seen enough of this foul sight. They progress toward the Third Pouch.

## Summary: Canto XIX

Dante already knows that the Third Pouch punishes the Simoniacs, those who bought or sold ecclesiastical pardons or offices. He decries the evil of simony before he and Virgil even view the pouch. Within, they see the sinners stuck headfirst in pits with only their feet protruding. As these souls writhe and flail in the pits, flames lap endlessly at their feet.

Dante notes one soul burning among flames redder than any others, and he goes to speak with him. The soul, that of Pope Nicholas III, first mistakes Dante for Boniface. After Dante corrects him, the soul tells Dante that he was a pope guilty of simony. He mourns his own position but adds that worse sinners than he still remain on Earth and await an even worse fate. Dante asserts that St. Peter did not pay Christ to receive the Keys of Heaven and Earth (which symbolize the papacy). He shows Nicholas no pity, saying that his punishment befits his grave sin. He then speaks out against all corrupt churchmen, calling them idolaters and an affliction on the world. Virgil approves of Dante's sentiments and helps Dante up over the ridge to the Fourth Pouch.

## SUMMARY: CANTO XX

In the Fourth Pouch, Dante sees a line of sinners trudging slowly along as if in a church procession. Seeing no apparent punishment other than this endless walking, he looks closer and finds, to his amazement, that each sinner's head points the wrong way—the souls' necks have been twisted so that their tears of pain now fall on their buttocks. Dante feels overcome by grief and pity, but Virgil rebukes him for his compassion.

As they pass by the Fourth Pouch, Virgil names several of the sinners here, who were Astrologers, Diviners, or Magicians in life. He explains the punishment of one specific sinner, saying that, since this individual wanted to use unholy powers to see ahead in life (that is, into the future), he has now been condemned to look backward for all of time. Virgil and Dante also see the sorceress Manto there, and Virgil relates a short tale of the founding of Mantua. They then continue on to the Fifth Pouch.

## ANALYSIS: CANTOS XVIII–XX

In life, the Panders and the Seducers in the First Pouch acted as slave drivers, moving women as merchandise from one buyer to the next. Now they run from one demon's whip to another's. The fate of the Flatterers is even more fitting, almost humorous in its allegorical suitability. For the excrement-lined pit they inhabit is, like these sycophants, "full of it." This coarse punishment demonstrates the great range of Dante's poetry, which encompasses both lofty rhetoric and scatology; like Geoffrey Chaucer, his near contemporary, Dante could appreciate the power of Scripture and still enjoy the humor of a dirty joke. He is equally at home recounting the classical legend of Jason and describing a scene fit for an earthy medieval comedy: "Searching it with my eyes / I saw one there whose head was so befouled / With shit, you couldn't tell which one he was"

(XVIII.106–108). This vulgarity marks a departure from the high, classical style of Virgil that Dante often echoes in *Inferno*.

In the scene with the Simoniacs, we find some of *Inferno*'s most biting criticisms of the Catholic Church. At the beginning of Canto XIX, before he and Virgil (or the readers) have even looked into the Third Pouch, Dante launches into an angry, six-line speech against these Simoniacs, followers of Simon Magus, a Samaritan sorcerer who tried to "buy" the gifts of the Holy Ghost. These lines underscore the moral intensity of the poem; however psychologically perceptive, imaginatively compelling, and emotionally affecting the poem may be, Dante always strives to separate good from evil and castigate vice in the name of justice. His moral diatribe to Pope Nicholas III contributes to this righteous tone. Serving as pope when Dante was only an adolescent (1277–1280), Nicholas was not Dante's greatest enemy in the Catholic Church. The diatribe here reflects not so much Dante's personal resentment of the man as his objection to certain church practices, which Nicholas represents.

Specifically, Dante condemns the Catholic Church's exchange of spiritual services for cash, especially in the granting of indulgences and in the reduction of penance, practices hotly condemned by Chaucer in *The Canterbury Tales*. It was this corruption that helped fuel Martin Luther's Protestant Reformation. Dante felt that church and state should have equal but separate powers; the church should have jurisdiction over the spiritual life but should avoid temporal power entirely. Hence, he has no sympathy for those churchmen who succumbed to the temptation of earthly wealth, alleging that they have transformed gold and silver into a god and thus have worshipped a false idol.

*Inferno* is rare among works of fiction in that it is not driven primarily by character. Insofar as Virgil and Dante the character emerge as fully realized human beings, they do not constitute especially complex figures, with Virgil generally embodying the traits of rationality and scrupulousness and Dante embodying those of sympathy and uncertainty. Their respective motivations throughout the story remain simple, even one-dimensional: Virgil acts according to his God-given duty of guiding Dante through Hell and offering him moral clarity; Dante generally acts only in response to the stimuli of the present moment, or out of the desire to traverse Hell safely.

What does drive *Inferno* is its progressive geography and moral symbolism; the poem's action arises as a result not of the traits and motives of Virgil and Dante but of their continuous forward motion through the different regions of Hell. Dante the character may develop somewhat over the course of *Inferno,* but only insofar as he learns to abhor sin and not pity its punishments, which are part of God's divine justice. The structure of this simple evolution generally parallels the story's linear narrative and geographical layout: the deeper Dante goes into Hell, the worse the sins and punishments become. Correspondingly, he becomes less likely to pity the suffering souls and more likely to repudiate them, as in the case of the Simoniacs in Canto XIX. This shift in Dante's behavior serves less to illumine Dante as a character and more to make moral statements.

## Cantos XXI–XXIII

### Summary: Canto XXI

Entering the Fifth Pouch of the Eighth Circle of Hell, Dante sees "an astounding darkness." The darkness is a great pit filled with a kind of boiling tar similar to what the Venetians used to patch their ships (XXI.6). As Dante examines the pitch to determine its composition, Virgil yells for him to watch out: a demon races up the rocks on the side of the pit, grabbing a new soul and tossing him into the blackness. As soon as the sinner comes up for breath, the demons below—the Malabranche, whose name means "evil claws"—thrust him back underneath with their prongs.

Virgil now advises Dante to hide behind a rock while he tries to negotiate their passage. The Malabranche at first act recalcitrant, but once he tells them that their journey is the will of Heaven, they agree to let the two travelers pass. They even provide an escort of ten demons—a necessary accompaniment, they say, as one of the bridges between the pouches has collapsed. Malacoda, the leader of the Malabranche (his name means "evil tail"), informs them of the exact moment that the bridge fell: 1,266 years, one day, and five hours before the present moment. Malacoda adds that a nearby ridge provides an alternate route.

### Summary: Canto XXII

The group goes forward, with Dante carefully watching the surface of the pitch for someone with whom to converse. He has few opportunities, as the sinners cannot stay out of the pitch long before getting skewered. Finally, Virgil manages to talk to one of the sinners who is being tortured outside of the pit. The soul, a Navarrese, explains that he served in the household of King Thibault and was sent to the Fifth Pouch because he accepted bribes—this pouch, then, contains the Barterers. The conversation breaks off as the tusked demon Ciriatto rips into the soul's body. Virgil then asks the soul if any Italians boil in the pitch. The soul replies that it could summon seven if the travelers wait for a moment. A nearby demon voices the suspicion that the soul merely intends to escape the demons' tortures and seek the relative relief of the pitch below. The other demons turn to listen to their coworker, and the soul races back to the pitch and dives in, not intending to return. Furious, two of the demons fly after the soul but become mired in the sticky blackness. As the other demons try to free their comrades, Virgil and Dante take the opportunity to make a discreet exit.

### Summary: Canto XXIII

As he and Virgil progress, Dante worries that they may have provoked the demons too much with this embarrassment. Virgil agrees. Suddenly, they hear the motion of wings and claws from behind, and turn to see the demons racing after them in a mad pack. Virgil acts quickly. Grabbing hold of Dante, he runs to the slope leading to the Sixth Pouch of the Eighth Circle of Hell. He then slides down the slope with Dante in his arms, thus foiling the demons, who may not leave their assigned pouch.

Now in the Sixth Pouch, Virgil and Dante see a group of souls trudging along in a circle, clothed in hats, cowls, and capes. Dante soon notices that lead lines their garments, rendering them massively heavy. One of the shades recognizes Dante's Tuscan speech and begs Dante to talk with him and his fellow sinners, as they include Italians in their ranks. These are the Hypocrites. The sight of one of them in particular stops Dante short: he lies crucified on the ground, and all of the other Hypocrites trample over him as they walk. The crucified sinner is Caiphus, who served as high priest under Pontius Pilate. Virgil asks one of the sinners for directions to the next part of Hell. He finds that Malacoda lied to him about the existence of a connecting ridge, and now learns the proper route.

---

### Analysis: Cantos XXI–XXIII

Although Malacoda intentionally misinforms Virgil and Dante about the passage along the ridge, his statement regarding the collapsed bridge appears truthful. The date he gives for its destruction matches that of the earthquake that Virgil describes in Canto XII. With this detail, Dante gives an elegant clue as to the timing of his journey: from it the reader may not only verify the year of this expedition as 1300 but also construe the specific day and hour during which it takes place. Malacoda says, "It was yesterday, five hours later than now, / That the twelve hundred and sixty-sixth year fell / Since the road here was ruined" (XXI.110–112). We know from Virgil's earlier comments that Hell shook with an earthquake not long before the Harrowing, or upon Christ's death. Figuring forward from Christ's death (according to the Gospels, with which Dante was familiar, Christ died at age thirty-three, at the hour of noon), we know that Dante's journey must have begun at midday on April 8, 1300—Good Friday. Thus, Dante follows Christ into Hell on the anniversary of His death, though the poet keeps this fact from the reader until the character has penetrated nearly to the bottom of the pit. As Dante leaves the Fifth Pouch, it is around seven in the morning on Holy Saturday, April 9.

The success of the Navarrese soul's trick on the two demons in Canto XXII comes as somewhat of a surprise. In general, the ministers of Hell seem too powerful to be duped by the sinners they so gleefully and effortlessly torture. One may account for the seeming anomaly in two ways. First, the demons are captives here too, as we realize in Canto XXIII when it is revealed that they cannot leave the Fifth Pouch. Just as every sinner is allotted a specific place, so are the demons—they are, after all, fallen angels, and have thus probably been given their own particular tortures for their disobedience to God. Second, the fact that these demons have erred and landed themselves in Hell points to their fallibility; such creatures may continue to make mistakes here in the underworld.

While the Navarrese soul manages to outsmart his torturers and win himself a sustained period of relief, it is important to note that other sinners also experience a respite from their sufferings—though only briefly—when Dante visits their circles. When the inhabitants of Hell speak with Dante, they step out of their tortures momentarily. Given the remarkable precision with which Dante the poet sketches out the complex rules that govern Hell, it seems paradoxical that the presence of Dante the character could lead to an interruption, albeit only temporary, of a sinner's eternal punishment. It creates no more of a paradox, however, than Dante's presence in Hell and ability to interact with the dead in the first place. Dante's presence in Hell, itself an exception to the rules, seems to upset Hell's equilibrium.

Dante's encounter with the crucified Caiphus constitutes a dramatic and moral highlight. Caiphus served as the high priest under Pontius Pilate, who advised the Pharisees to allow Jesus to die rather than provoke trouble in the nation. His punishment bears a threefold allegorical significance: because he was a hypocrite, preaching prudence but not showing it, he resides in the Sixth Pouch; because he called for Christ's crucifixion, he himself lies crucified; and because his actions contributed to the suffering of one for the sins of many, he now bears the weight of all of the other lead-laden Hypocrites.

Dante continues to use his gift for symbolism to make moral points about the sinners of myth and history, rendering this section the most ominous and grotesque so far. As the poets progress ever closer to Satan, their surroundings grow darker and more dangerous, to the extent that they only barely escape attack by the demons in Canto XXIII. Only Virgil's bizarre use of his own body as a sled saves Dante from the rampaging demons—surely one of the strangest chase scenes in all of literature.

## Cantos XXIV–XXVI

### Summary: Canto XXIV
Making their way to the Seventh Pouch of the Eighth Circle of Hell, Virgil and Dante face many dangers. Because of the collapsed bridge, they must navigate treacherous rocks, and Virgil carefully selects a path before helping his mortal companion along. Dante loses his breath for a moment, but Virgil urges him onward, indicating that a long climb still awaits them. They descend the wall into the Seventh Pouch, where teeming masses of serpents chase after naked sinners; coiled snakes bind the sinners' hands and legs. Dante watches a serpent catch one of the sinners and bite him between the shoulders. He watches in amazement as the soul instantly catches fire and burns up, then rises from the ashes to return to the pit of serpents.

Virgil speaks to this soul, who identifies himself as a Tuscan, Vanni Fucci, whom Dante knew on Earth. Fucci tells them that he was put here for robbing a sacristy—the Seventh Pouch holds Thieves. Angered that Dante is witnessing his miserable condition, he foretells the defeat of Dante's political party, the White Guelphs, at Pistoia.

### Summary: Canto XXV
Cursing God with an obscene gesture, Fucci flees with serpents coiling around him, and Dante now relishes the sight. Moving further along the pit, he and Virgil behold an even more incredible scene. Three souls cluster just beneath them, and a giant, six-footed serpent wraps itself so tightly around one of them that its form merges

with that of its victim; the serpent and soul become a single creature. As the other souls watch in horror, another reptile bites one of them in the belly. The soul and the reptile stare at each other, transfixed, as the reptile slowly takes on the characteristics of the man and the man takes on those of the reptile. Soon they have entirely reversed their forms.

## SUMMARY: CANTO XXVI

Having recognized these thieves as Florentines, Dante sarcastically praises Florence for earning such widespread fame not only on Earth but also in Hell. Virgil now leads him along the ridges to the Eighth Pouch, where they see numerous flames flickering in a deep, dark valley. Coming closer, Virgil informs Dante that each flame contains a sinner. Dante sees what appear to be two souls contained together in one flame, and Virgil identifies them as Ulysses and Diomedes, both suffering for the same fraud committed in the Trojan War.

Dante desires to speak with these warriors, but Virgil, warning him that the Greeks might disdain Dante's medieval Italian, speaks to them as an intermediary. He succeeds in getting Ulysses to tell them about his death. Restlessly seeking new challenges, he sailed beyond the western edge of the Mediterranean, which was believed to constitute the rim of the Earth; legend asserted that death awaited any mariner venturing beyond that point. After five months, he and his crew came in view of a great mountain. Before they could reach it, however, a great storm arose and sank their ship.

## ANALYSIS: CANTOS XXIV–XXVI

Early in Canto XXIV, Dante clarifies the geographical structure of Malebolge (the Eighth Circle): it slopes continuously downward, so that, after the Tenth Pouch, it runs right into Hell's central pit. Virgil and Dante have thus not been simply progressing around the underworld's circumference but descending deeper and deeper into the Earth's core.

Virgil emphasizes the importance of fame when he urges Dante to persevere through the difficult descent, telling him that only persistence can win a person fame and glory. We have seen Dante the poet ascribe great importance to earthly fame before, particularly in the figures of the several shades who have asked Dante to recall their names and stories on Earth. This concern for the preservation of one's legacy represents one of Dante's most surprising departures from conventional medieval Christian morality: Christ urged His disciples to shun worldly glory and focus themselves on the glory of God's Kingdom. In Dante's mind, however, the two are intimately connected: as long as one's glory arises from honest work, it can improve one's lot in the afterlife. One encounters this notion more frequently in classical Greek and Roman poetry than in medieval Christian texts; its inclusion here underscores *The Comedy*'s debt to classical tradition (though, in general, Dante's attitude toward the ancients remains ambiguous; ensuing passages contain rebukes of the old civilization).

While Dante notes that fame stemming from honest achievements can benefit a soul for eternity, he warns that fame stemming from crime earns the criminal no happiness. The poet makes this point with the figure of Vanni Fucci, who is the first sinner to ask that Dante *not* spread his story on Earth. He cringes with shame when Dante sees him, and, unlike the other sinners, would prefer not to interact with the traveler. Fucci's singularity lies also in his defiance, as Dante notes: the shade obscenely gestures into the sky.

Amidst his discussions of fame and reputation, Dante takes the opportunity to advance his own glory. Never modest about his own poetic gifts, he uses the power of these scenes to support his claim of superiority over the ancient poets. He devises an affecting and grotesquely fitting penalty for the Thieves: having stolen in life, they must constantly steal one another's forms and constantly have their own forms stolen from them. He portrays the punishment with vivid language and imaginative detail. Halfway through his description of these horrors, however, Dante declares outright that he has outdone both Ovid and Lucan in his ability to write scenes of metamorphosis and transformation. (Ovid's *Metamorphoses* focuses entirely on transformations; Lucan wrote the *Pharsalia,* an account of the Roman political transition and turmoil in the first century B.C.) Dante touts both his ingenuity in envisioning these monstrous transformations and his poetic skill in rendering them. In both aspects, he claims to surpass two of the classical poets most renowned for their mythological inventions and vivid imagery, thus again attempting to subsume the classical tradition within his own poem. These claims hearken back to the subtle note of self-congratulation that Dante includes in Canto IV, when he meets these poets face to face; his attitude toward them combines respect and condescension.

In Canto XXVI, Dante makes another strike at antiquity by placing its last remaining hero, Ulysses (known as Odysseus to the Greeks), in the Eighth Pouch of the Eighth Circle of Hell. Dante explains Ulysses' presence in this section of Hell by referencing his role in the ruse of the Trojan Horse, which enabled the sacking of Troy by the Achaeans. But Dante probably had a number of different motivations for placing Ulysses so deep in Hell. First, we have seen that Dante reveres Rome; Ulysses, as an enemy of Aeneas, who later founded Rome, can be seen as an enemy of Rome as well. Dante may be reaping revenge on him. Additionally, he may intend the great Greek hero's spiritual defeat here to remind readers of the Greeks' eventual defeat by the Romans on Earth. But, as evidenced by his dismissal of Lucan and Ovid in the previous canto, Dante finds that even Roman antiquity contains flaws. Here, he implies that the advent of Christianity has constituted an invaluable improvement for civilization: notwithstanding his honored place within Greek and Roman tradition, Ulysses behaved recklessly and fraudulently by Christian standards, and, in Dante's Hell, Christian morals always take precedence over ancient values.

## Cantos XXVII–XXIX

### Summary: Canto XXVII

After hearing Ulysses' story, Virgil and Dante start down their path again, only to be stopped by another flame-immersed soul. This soul lived in Italy's Romagna region, and now, hearing Dante speak the Lombard tongue, he asks for news of his homeland. Dante replies that Romagna suffers under violence and tyranny but not outright war. He then asks the soul his name, and the sinner, believing that Dante will never leave the abyss and thus will be unable to spread word of his infamy, consents to tell him.

He introduces himself as Guido da Montefeltro and states that he was originally a member of the Ghibellines. After a time, he underwent a religious conversion and joined a Franciscan monastery, but he was then persuaded by Pope Boniface VIII to reenter politics on the opposing side. At one point, Boniface asked him for advice on how to conquer Palestrina (formerly called Penestrino, it served as the fortress of the Ghibelline Colonna family). Da Montefeltro showed reluctance, but Boniface promised him absolution in advance, even if his counsel were to prove wrong. He then agreed to give his advice, which turned out to be incorrect. When he died, St. Francis came for him, but a devil pulled him away, saying that a man could not receive absolution before sinning, for absolution cannot precede repentance and repentance cannot precede the sin.

Such preemptive absolution he deemed "contradictory," and thus invalid. Calling himself a logician, the devil took da Montefeltro to Minos, who deemed the sinner guilty of fraudulent counsel and assigned him to the Eighth Pouch of the Eighth Circle of Hell.

## SUMMARY: CANTO XXVIII

Virgil and Dante continue on to the Ninth Pouch, where they see a line of souls circling perpetually. Dante sees they bear wounds worse than those suffered at the battles at Troy and Ceparano. A devil stands at one point of the circle with a sword, splitting open each sinner who walks by. One of the sinners speaks to Dante as he passes—it is Mohammed, prophet of the Muslims. These are the Sowers of Scandal and Schism, and for their sins of division they themselves are split apart. Worse, as they follow the circle around, their wounds close up so that they are whole by the time they come back to the sword, only to be struck again.

Many others in this line look up at Dante, hearing his living voice. The Italians among them beg Dante to carry messages to certain men still living on Earth. They make predictions of a shipwreck and give a warning for Fra Dolcino, who is in danger of joining them when he dies. Finally, Dante sees a man carrying his own head in his hands: it is Bertran de Born, who advised a young king to rebel against his father.

## SUMMARY: CANTO XXIX

Virgil reprimands Dante for staring so long at the wounded souls, reminding him that their time is limited; this time, however, Dante stubbornly follows his own inclination. He takes note of one more soul, an ancestor of his who died unavenged.

Finally, Virgil and Dante follow the ridge down and to the left until they can see the Tenth Pouch below them. This pouch houses the Falsifiers, and it is divided into four zones. In the First Zone, souls huddle in heaps and sprawl out on the ground. Scabs cover them from head to foot; they scratch at them furiously and incessantly.

Dante locates two Italians in this zone. Since his journey will take him back to the world of the living, he offers to spread their names among men if they will tell him their stories. The two souls oblige. One of them is Griffolino of Arezzo, who was burned at the stake for heresy but has landed here in the Tenth Pouch for his practice of the occult art of alchemy. The other is a Florentine, Capocchio, who was likewise an alchemist burned at the stake. We learn that the First Zone holds the Falsifiers of Metals.

## ANALYSIS: CANTOS XXVII–XXIX

Although Dante's discussion of the Italians in his Hell aims to point out their political wrongs, he frequently acknowledges their possession of what he deems a minor, if misguided, virtue—that of patriotism. We see in the Eighth and Ninth Pouches how many Italians, like Farinata and Cavalcanti in Canto X, retain their concern for their homeland even after death. Da Montefeltro pleads desperately for news about Romagna, despite the fact that no news, however good, could possibly bring him peace of mind. Dante seems to take pride in the devotion of his compatriots to their fatherland, for their concern speaks to the glory of the nation and the fidelity of Italians.

Da Montefeltro's tale about his dealings with Boniface establishes a theological point and allows Dante to apply one of his Aristotelian convictions to Catholic doctrine. Although Boniface had given da Montefeltro absolution according to the proper rite, Dante still holds him accountable for his sin. He does so not because he does not believe in the true power of confession or because he thinks Boniface's corruption renders him unable to absolve sins; rather, the absolution fails because it violates the fundamental Aristotelian principle of contradiction—that an entity cannot simultaneously be both of a specific nature and not of that specific nature. Absolution from sin requires one to be repentant; absolution received before a sin has been committed proves invalid because, at the moment that absolution is being issued, the person still intends to commit the sin—indicating a lack of repentance. Dante's invocation of Aristotelian philosophy speaks to his belief in the importance of reason in moral decision-making. He implies that Christians who find themselves in moral dilemmas must use their reason rather than blindly follow the directions of a church figure. Dante does not question here the spiritual authority of the church, to which he shows steadfast respect throughout *Inferno*. However, he does not believe that this authority should overrule logic—especially given the church's frequent descent into corruption. The devil's reference to himself as a logician invokes the idea of the indisputability of divine justice.

The opening of Canto XXVIII, which describes the wounds of the Sowers of Scandal and Schism, instances Dante's effective use in *The Comedy* of starkly contrasting styles. He opens the canto by stating that no one would be able to properly describe what he saw there and that anyone who tried to do so would certainly fall short. He goes on, nevertheless, to use a mixture of the high classical mode and the low medieval idiom to present the image compellingly. He begins with allusions to great historical battles, such as those at Troy, claiming that the wounds suffered during these Trojan battles, which Virgil catalogued in the *Aeneid,* pale in comparison to the wounds he now glimpses. This manner of referencing events from epics and other legends characterized much of classical literature. Just a few lines later, however, Dante enters into a realistic catalogue of the wounds, complete with scatological references to "the farting-place" and "shit" (XXVIII.25–28). Drawing on the nobility of classical tales of war, while also evoking the earthly physicality of medieval comedy, Dante creates a doubly intense impression of violence, at once both epic and visceral, lofty and penetrating.

The request of the Italian souls in the Ninth Pouch that Dante bring warnings back to certain living men seems an attempt, like that made by the souls who ask Dante to spread their names, to forge some sort of existence outside of Hell. To be in contact with the mortal world would allow them to escape, in some small way, the eternal, atemporal realm that they now occupy. But the character Dante does not oblige them, for spiritual reasons. In the New Testament, God refused the rich man in Hell who wanted to have Lazarus go back to Earth and warn his sons about their sinful lives. Perhaps fearful of seeming presumptuous, the character Dante makes no answer to their request. Of course, the poet Dante seems to have his own agenda; his poem takes the recounting of their stories as a central part of its project.

## Cantos XXX–XXXIII

### Summary: Canto XXX

Beholding the Second Zone in the Tenth Pouch of the Eighth Circle of Hell, Dante recalls stories of antiquity in which great suffering caused humans to turn on each other like animals. But the viciousness portrayed in these stories pales in comparison with what he witnesses here, where the sinners tear at each other with their teeth; these are the Falsifiers of Others' Persons. Dante sees a woman, Myrrha, who lusted after her father and disguised herself as another in order to gratify her lust. Some of the sinners of the Third Zone, the Falsifiers of Coins, mingle among these souls. Dante speaks with Master Adam, who counterfeited Florentine money; part of his punishment is to be racked with thirst. Adam points out two members of the Fourth Zone, the Falsifiers of Words, or Liars: one is the wife of Potiphar, who falsely accused Joseph of trying to seduce her, and the other is a Greek man, Sinon. The latter apparently knows Adam and comes over to pick a fight with him. Dante listens to them bicker for a while. Virgil harshly reprimands his companion, telling him that it is demeaning to listen to such a petty disagreement.

## SUMMARY: CANTO XXXI

As Virgil and Dante finally approach the pit in the center of the Eighth Circle of Hell, Dante sees what appear to be tall towers in the mist. Going closer, he realizes that they are actually giants standing in the pit. Their navels are level with the Eighth Circle, but their feet stand in the Ninth Circle, at the very bottom of Hell. One of the giants begins to speak in gibberish; he is Nimrod, who, via his participation in building the Tower of Babel, brought the confusion of different languages to the world.

Virgil names some of the other giants whom they pass until they come to Antaeus, the one who will help them down the pit. After listening to Virgil's request, Antaeus takes the two travelers in one of his enormous hands and slowly sets them down by his feet, at the base of the enormous well. They are now in the Ninth Circle of Hell, the realm of Traitors.

## SUMMARY: CANTO XXXII

Dante feels that he cannot adequately express the grim terror of what he and Virgil see next, but he states that he will nevertheless make an attempt. Walking past the giant's feet, the two come upon a vast frozen lake, as clear as glass—Cocytus. In the ice, souls stand frozen up to their heads, their teeth chattering. The First Ring of the Ninth Circle of Hell is called Caina (after Cain, who, as Genesis recounts, slew his brother, Abel), where traitors to their kin receive their punishment. Virgil and Dante see twins frozen face to face, butting their heads against each other in rage. Walking farther, Dante accidentally kicks one of the souls in the cheek. Leaning down to apologize, he thinks he recognizes the face—it turns out to belong to Bocca degli Abati, an Italian traitor. Dante threatens Bocca and tears out some of his hair before leaving him in the ice. Virgil and Dante progress to the Second Ring, Antenora, which contains those who betrayed their homeland or party. Continuing across the lake, Dante is horrified to see one sinner gnawing at another's head from behind. He inquires into the sin that warranted such cruelty, stating that he might be able to spread the gnawing sinner's good name on Earth.

## Summary: Canto XXXIII

*I did not open them—for to be rude*
*To such a one as him was courtesy.*

*(See* QUOTATIONS, *p. 72)*

The sinner raises himself from his gnawing and declares that in life he was Count Ugolino; the man whose head he chews was Archbishop Ruggieri. Both men lived in Pisa, and the archbishop, a traitor himself, had imprisoned Ugolino and his sons as traitors. He denied them food, and when the sons died, Ugolino, in his hunger, was driven to eat the flesh of their corpses.

Dante now rails against Pisa, a community known for its scandal but that nevertheless has remained unpunished on Earth. He and Virgil then pass to the Third Ring, Ptolomea, which houses those who betrayed their guests. The souls here lie on their backs in the frozen lake, with only their faces poking out of the ice. Dante feels a cold wind sweeping across the lake, and Virgil tells him that they will soon behold its source.

The poets react with particular horror at the sight of the next two souls in the Third Ring, those of Fra Alberigo and Branca d'Oria. Although these individuals have not yet died on Earth, their crimes were so great that their souls were obliged to enter Hell before their time; devils occupy their living bodies aboveground. After leaving these shades, Virgil and Dante approach the Fourth Ring of the Ninth Circle of Hell, the very bottom of the pit.

## Analysis: Cantos XXX–XXXIII

Although Myrrha's sin was one of lust, which should situate her in the Second Circle of Hell, she appears in the Eighth Circle of Hell because she concealed her true identity in pursuing that lust, thus committing a sin of fraud. This technicality reveals something about Dante's technique. The incestuous woman's punishment implies that one is chastised according to one's greatest sin; such a rule fails to hold for Dido, however, who committed suicide because of love but was put with the Lustful rather than with the Suicides. Dante is not trying to make a theological point with this seeming incongruity; rather, as a storyteller, he places sinners according to the sin that their respective stories most embody. Potiphar's wife, for example, is famous for the biblical passage in which she tries to seduce Joseph and then falsely accuses him of trying to seduce her. It is not her lust that makes the story striking but her lie about it; thus, Dante places her with the liars. Though *Inferno* often proves rigidly exact in following its self-created rules, at other times Dante simply follows his narrative instinct.

Although Virgil has been gently hurrying Dante along throughout *Inferno,* his exasperated outburst at the end of Canto XXX comes as a surprise. His forceful admonition responds not merely to Dante's tarrying but also to its motivation: Virgil here warns both Dante and the reader that the desire to witness Hell and know about its inhabitants must not become a form of voyeurism—we should not watch torture merely for the sake of watching it. The reminder creates a certain sense of irony, for Dante the poet often encourages voyeurism in his readers, using spectacular imaginative effects and dramatic imagery to hold our interest. Indeed, the poem has endured in large part because of its appeal to human sentiments and to the imagination; in this indulgence, it furthers voyeurism more than it contributes to any quest for moral understanding. Still, Dante continues to place moral issues at the center of his work, and the character Dante's abashed correction of his behavior emphasizes the poet's sense of priorities.

After being lowered down to Cocytus by the giant Antaeus, Dante claims that he cannot adequately portray what he sees, saying that he lacks the "harsh and grating rhymes" to depict this section of Hell (XXXII.1). By "harsh and grating rhymes" he means jarring poetic sounds—literally, abrasive-sounding words and phrases, which would best convey the starkness of the scene before him in the frozen lake. This statement reveals a great deal about Dante's attitude toward poetry, which he implies should be beautiful and balanced rather than strident or discordant. The horror of Hell is no subject for the melody and metaphor of the high classical style. But Dante's protestations ring of false modesty; scenes throughout *Inferno* evidence his mastery of the mixed style. He repeatedly proves just as capable with low style—which he uses here with great skill, painting a truly haunting picture—as he is with high style.

Here, in the lowest circle of Hell, Dante finally encounters a sinner who shows no interest in him—Bocca degli Abati, who betrayed the Florentine Guelphs in battle. Degli Abati tells Dante to leave him alone, but Dante cannot hold back his contempt for this traitor to his party, illustrating both his own loyalty to the Guelphs and his increasing inability to pity the punishments of sinners. Despite Dante's occasional cynicism toward all politics—a result, in part, of his exile—we see now that he remains true to his party, the Guelphs, and that political concerns still weigh heavily on his mind and his emotions.

By placing the still-living Fra Alberigo and Branca d'Oria in Hell, Dante commits his greatest breach of orthodox Catholic theology in *Inferno*. The notion of a sinner's soul being placed in Hell prior to his or her physical death diverges radically from Catholic doctrine; whereas Dante intends many of his scenes as illustrations of Christian morals, his purposes in this scene clearly lie elsewhere. Most likely, he means to emphasize the gravity of Alberigo's and d'Oria's crimes; perhaps, too, he aims to add some humor to this penultimate canto. It would not be out of character for this poem, which interweaves wildly varying styles, to incorporate a bit of ironic comedy just before the dramatic climax: the approach of Lucifer himself.

## CANTO XXXIV

### SUMMARY: CANTO XXXIV

Still journeying toward the center of the Ninth Circle of Hell, Dante becomes aware of a great shape in the distance, hidden by the fog. Right under his feet, however, he notices sinners completely covered in ice, sometimes several feet deep, contorted into various positions. These souls constitute the most evil of all sinners—the Traitors to their Benefactors. Their part of Hell, the Fourth Ring of the Ninth Circle, is called Judecca.

Dante and Virgil advance toward the giant, mist-shrouded shape. As they approach through the fog, they behold its true form. The sight unnerves Dante to such an extent that he knows not whether he is alive or dead. The figure is Lucifer, Dis, Satan—no one name does justice to his terrible nature. The size of his arms alone exceeds all of the giants of the Eighth Circle of Hell put together. He stands in the icy lake, his torso rising above the surface. Gazing upward, Dante sees that Lucifer has three horrible faces, one looking straight ahead and the others looking back over his shoulders. Beneath each head rises a set of wings, which wave back and forth, creating the icy winds that keep Cocytus frozen.

Each of Lucifer's mouths holds a sinner—the three greatest sinners of human history, all Traitors to a Benefactor. In the center mouth dangles Judas Iscariot, who betrayed Christ. In the left and right mouths hang Brutus and Cassius, who murdered Julius Caesar in the Roman Senate. Brutus and Cassius appear with their heads out, but Judas is lodged headfirst; only his twitching legs protrude.

The mouths chew their victims, constantly tearing the traitors to pieces but never killing them. Virgil tells Dante that they have now seen all of Hell and must leave at once.

Putting Dante on his back, Virgil performs a startling feat. He avoids the flapping wings and climbs onto Lucifer's body, gripping the Devil's frozen tufts of hair and lowering himself and his companion down. Underneath Cocytus, they reach Lucifer's waist, and here Virgil slowly turns himself around, climbing back upward. However, Dante notes with amazement that Lucifer's legs now rise above them, his head below. Virgil explains that they have just passed the center of the Earth: when Lucifer fell from Heaven, he plunged headfirst into the planet; his body stuck here in the center. According to Virgil, the impact caused the lands of the Southern Hemisphere to retreat to the North, leaving only the Mountain of Purgatory in the water of the South. Dante and Virgil climb a long path through this hemisphere, until they finally emerge to see the stars again on the opposite end of the Earth from where they began.

## ANALYSIS: CANTO XXXIV

Here in the Fourth Ring of the Ninth Circle of Hell, at the utter bottom, Dante comes to the end of his hierarchy of sins and thus completes the catalogue of evil that dominates and defines *Inferno*. Although *Inferno* explores most explicitly the theme of divine retribution and justice, the poem's unrelenting descriptions, categorizations, and analysis of sin makes human evil its fundamental subject. The positioning of fraud as the worst of sins helps us to define evil: fraud, more than any other crime, acts contrary to God's greatest gift to mankind—love. A deed's degree of wickedness thus depends on the degree to which it opposes love. So-called ordinary fraud only breaks the natural bonds of trust and love that form between men; other categories of fraud reach an even greater depth of evil because they break an additional bond of love. Of these, frauds against kin, country, and guests constitute the lighter end of the scale, for they violate only socially obligated bonds—our culture expects us to love our family and our homeland and to be a good host. But fraud against a benefactor constitutes the worst fraud of all, according to Dante, for it violates a love that is purely voluntary, a love that most resembles God's love for us. Correspondingly, one who betrays one's benefactor comes closest to betraying God directly. Thus, the ultimate sinner, Judas Iscariot, was a man who betrayed both simultaneously, for his benefactor was Jesus Christ.

The justice of Brutus and Cassius's placement in the lowest depths of Hell is more problematic. History tells us that these men did betray and murder Julius Caesar, but Caesar's status as a great benefactor remains disputed. The explanation for their presence lies in Dante's often-implied belief that Rome is the sovereign city, destined to rule the world both physically and spiritually. Just as Christ, whose church is centered in Rome, was the perfect manifestation of religion, Dante feels that Caesar was the perfect manifestation of secular government, as the emperor of Rome at the height of its power. Since spiritual concerns must, in the end, outweigh temporal ones, Judas has committed the greater sin, and his head, rather than his legs, feels the constant chewing of Lucifer's teeth. However, the fact that Brutus and Cassius suffer a punishment only slightly less harsh demonstrates Dante's belief that church and state play equally important roles, each in its own sphere. Throughout *Inferno*, Dante has expressed the view that church and state should remain separate but equal. Now, Dante finds an arrangement for the final circle of Hell that both completes his vision of the moral hierarchy and makes one last, vivid assertion of his politics.

Dante's portrait of Lucifer makes him a grotesque mimicry of God in Heaven, much in the same way that the sinners' punishments in Hell grotesquely mimic their sins on Earth. We recall that the poem refers earlier to Hell as a city—a perversion of the city of God. In the same way, Lucifer, with his three heads in one body, constitutes a perversion of the Trinity, the three aspects of the single God. Medieval Christian theology held that evil can only mimic or distort, not create; Lucifer is Dante's embodiment of this premise.

Dante displays a surprisingly astute grasp of physics in describing Virgil and Dante's transition between the Northern and Southern Hemispheres. Using Virgil as a mouthpiece, he describes the center of the Earth as the point to which all weight falls. This depiction, and Virgil and Dante's turnabout at the center, forms a fairly accurate account of gravity; such an understanding eluded many of Dante's contemporaries. The fanciful explanation of how Lucifer ended up at the center of the Earth demonstrates a somewhat less keen comprehension of the world, however: Dante, along with most fourteenth-century thinkers, believed that the Southern Hemisphere contained no continents.

## ADDENDUM: TERZA RIMA

One of the most important aesthetic features of Dante's *Divine Comedy* receives little discussion among readers of the poem's English translations: Dante's poetic form, the terza rima, which scholars believe him to have invented for *The Comedy*. Terza rima utilizes three-line stanzas, which combine iambic meter with a propulsive rhyme scheme. Within each stanza, the first and third lines rhyme, the middle line having a different end sound; the end sound of this middle line then rhymes with the first and third lines of the next stanza. The rhyme scheme thus runs *aba bcb cdc ded efe,* and so forth. Shelley's "Ode to the West Wind" (1820) instances one of the finest uses of terza rima in an English-language poem:

> *O wild West Wind, thou breath of Autumn's being,*
> *Thou, from whose unseen presence the leaves dead*
> *Are driven, like ghosts from an enchanter fleeing,*
>
> *Yellow, and black, and pale, and hectic red,*
> *Pestilence-stricken multitudes: O thou,*
> *Who chariotest to their dark wintry bed*

Because this rhyme scheme could propagate itself forever, a terza rima poem typically ends with a stanza of only one line, which rhymes with the middle line of the second to last stanza. We see this type of close in Canto XXXIII of *Inferno*:

> *For with Romagna's worst spirit I have found*
> *One of you—already, for deeds he was guilty of,*
> *Bathed in Cocytus: in soul now underground*
>
> *Who in body still appears alive, above.*

The English language possesses a vocabulary more massive than that of Italian: because English is descended more or less equally from three different languages (Latin, Anglo-Saxon, and medieval French), it contains many synonyms. The word *kingly,* for instance, descends from Anglo-Saxon, while *regal* comes from Latin and *royal* comes from French. Despite this abundance of words, English provides far fewer possibilities for rhyme than Italian, which stems much more directly from Latin, a language that contains regimented systems for noun and verb endings. Nouns in Italian are thus much more likely to rhyme with one another than nouns in English; the same holds true for verbs.

As a result, writing terza rima stanzas, which depend so heavily on available rhymes, proves punishingly difficult in English. To circumvent this difficulty, most translators of *The Divine Comedy* sidestep the terza rima form, choosing to translate either in prose or unrhymed blank verse. Some translators utilize rhyme, but among recent translations, only Robert Pinsky's makes an attempt to preserve Dante's verse form. In order to do so, Pinsky makes liberal use of half-rhymes ("near"/"fire," "alive"/"move"), and often departs widely from Dante's original lines—most of his cantos contain fewer lines than Dante's.

For these reasons, a discussion of terza rima does not always seem relevant for English-language readers. Nevertheless, an analysis of Dante's reasons for using terza rima helps us to understand better both his style and his themes, two elements that figure strongly in English readers' appreciation of the poem.

Dante's use of terza rima underscores the intricate connections among story, form, and theme in *Inferno,* an unprecedented and unmatched unity of parts that is probably Dante's greatest poetic achievement. First, as the rhyme scheme passes new rhymes from one stanza to the next, it creates a feeling of effortless forward motion. This dynamic matches the endless advance of Dante and Virgil as they descend into Hell, an advance that drives the plot. Second, terza rima, with its three-line stanzas, reflects other groupings of threes found throughout Dante's poem, all of which contribute to a complex symbolism. The number three plays an important role in Catholic theology because of the triune God, made up of the Father, Son, and Holy Ghost. In *Inferno,* Dante encounters three beasts in the first canto; three holy women send Virgil to guide him; Satan has three heads and chews on three sinners. By using terza rima, Dante makes a thematic element into a structural building block as well. Terza rima also serves to link the poem's smaller formal structure to its larger geometry, for the three-line stanzas mirror the three-pronged nature of the entire *Divine Comedy,* which comprises *Inferno, Purgatorio,* and *Paradiso.* Furthermore, each of these parts contains its own three sections: in *Inferno,* for instance, these are the Ante-Inferno, Upper Hell, and Lower Hell. *Purgatorio* and *Paradiso* each have thirty-three cantos; although *Inferno* has thirty-four, its first canto acts as a general prologue to *The Comedy* as a whole. Hell, in its entirety, divides into nine circles—three times three. Many more threesomes exist as well, illuminating only a small part of the intricacies of Dante's structural plan.

# IMPORTANT QUOTATIONS EXPLAINED

1.  Midway on our life's journey, I found myself
    In dark woods, the right road lost.

These famous lines, narrated by Dante, open *Inferno* and immediately establish the allegorical plane on which the story's meaning unfolds (I.1–2). The use of such potent words as "journey" and "right road" signifies the religious aspect of Dante's impending adventure and quickly notifies us that we are leaving the realm of the literal. Likewise, the image of being lost in "dark woods" sets up a clear dichotomy between the unenlightened ignorance involved in a lack of faith in God and the clear radiance provided by God's love. The simple contrast between the "dark woods," which embody Dante's fear, and the "right road," which embodies Dante's confidence in God, makes his challenge clear—he sets out to look for God in a sinful world. His reference to "our life" contributes to the allegorical level of *Inferno*: the journey upon which Dante is embarking is not solely his but rather that of every human being. He describes his journey in only the vaguest of terms, with no mention of where he is coming from or where he is heading, because he believes that this journey is one that every individual undertakes so as to understand his or her sins and find his or her peace with God.

2.   *through me you enter into the city of woes*
     *through me you enter into eternal pain,*
     *through me you enter the population of loss.*
       . . .
     *abandon all hope, you who enter here.*

Dante reads these lines, which he finds inscribed on the Gate of
Hell, as he and Virgil pass into the Ante-Inferno before the river
Acheron in Canto III (III.1–7). These lines may be said to represent
the voice of Hell, as they declare its nature, origin, and purpose, and
thus pave the way for what is to come throughout the poem. First,
the inscription portrays Hell as a city, which defines much of the
geography of the poem—Hell is a geographically contained area
bound by walls and containing a vast population of souls. Hell is
thus a grotesque counterpart to Heaven, which Virgil describes as
the city of God. Second, the inscription portrays Hell as a place of
eternal woes, pain, and loss, situating it as the center of God's strict
punishment of sinners, a place from which there is supposed to be
no escape ("ABANDON ALL HOPE").

QUOTATIONS

3.          . . . One day, for pleasure,
          We read of Lancelot, by love constrained:
          Alone, suspecting nothing, at our leisure.

          . . .

          And so was he who wrote it; that day we read

          . . .

          No further. . . .

Francesca speaks these lines in Canto V when she tells Dante the story of her love affair with Paolo, her husband's brother, for which they are now both condemned to the tempest of the Second Circle of Hell (V.112–124). Francesca describes how she and Paolo, who had fallen secretly in love, read to one another from a story about Lancelot and Guinevere, who also shared an illicit love (Guinevere was King Arthur's wife). Feeling that their own story was reflected in the story of the Arthurian lovers, Paolo and Francesca were overcome with emotion, and when they read about Lancelot and Guinevere's first kiss, Paolo kissed Francesca; Francesca's husband, spying on the lovers, had them killed before they had the opportunity to repent and seek God's forgiveness.

This passage, in addition to being one of the most famous in *Inferno,* is one of the most moving. Dante heightens the tragic quality of the romance between Paolo and Francesca with his mastery of the style of romantic love poetry—one of the many modes that he assumes in *Inferno.* These lines also imply the power of literature to excite the emotions, a power that Dante hoped to harness. Perhaps most important, they offer a sympathetic story to explain the suffering of these souls in Hell, allowing the reader to share Dante's compassion for them. As the poem progresses, the stories told by the damned souls grow less and less sympathetic, compelling the reader to share Dante's growing abhorrence of sin and underscoring the poem's theme that sin is not to be pitied.

QUOTATIONS

4.  I did not open them—for to be rude
    To such a one as him was courtesy.

Dante speaks these lines in reference to a promise, in Canto XXXIII, to open Fra Alberigo's eyes for him (XXXIII.146–147). Alberigo, one of the living men who was snatched and brought to Hell before they died because of the magnitude of their sins, is lying supine in Cocytus, the frozen lake; his tears have frozen over his eyes, and he has asked Dante to remove the rings of ice from his eyes so that he might cry freely for a time. Dante initially agrees, but after he realizes the extent of the man's evil, he changes his mind and recants his promise, taking pleasure in Alberigo's suffering. This quote is extremely important to Dante's overall development in the poem, indicating the extent to which he learns not to pity suffering sinners and to despise sin wholeheartedly. At the beginning of *Inferno*, Dante weeps for many of the suffering souls; by the penultimate canto, he doesn't even help them weep for themselves. This attitude, wholly endorsed by Virgil, may seem harsh to the modern reader, but it is portrayed in *Inferno* as Dante's necessary first step toward overcoming sin in his own life and finding salvation in God.

QUOTATIONS

5.    To get back up to the shining world from there
      My guide and I went into that hidden tunnel;
      . . .
      Where we came forth, and once more saw the stars.

These concluding words of *Inferno* describe Dante and Virgil's climb out of the underworld and back to the surface of the Earth (XXXIV.134–140). Dante the poet fancies that when Lucifer was flung down from Heaven, he struck the Earth in a place exactly opposite Jerusalem in the Southern Hemisphere and penetrated the center of the planet; the cavity left by his fall is Hell. As Dante and Virgil climb out of Hell on the other side of the world, they climb up through a cavity that was once full of earth; the earth was displaced by Lucifer's fall and thrust up to the surface, where it formed an island. This island is Purgatory, which Dante tours in the next part of *The Divine Comedy, Purgatorio,* as he continues his trek toward salvation.

   These lines are chiefly important because of how they end: Dante, fresh from his nightmarish visit to Hell, gazes up at Heaven's stars. This image symbolizes the idea that Dante has begun his slow climb out of sin and confusion and has taken a step toward Beatrice and God, ending this very dark poem on a note of brilliant optimism. It is greatly significant that both *Purgatorio* and *Paradiso* end with the same word as *Inferno*: *stele,* or the stars. It is clear not only that Dante aspires to Heaven but also that his poem aspires to a place among the epics.

QUOTATIONS

# KEY FACTS

FULL TITLE
*Inferno*

AUTHOR
Dante Alighieri

TYPE OF WORK
Narrative poem

GENRE
Epic poem, religious allegory, fantasy

LANGUAGE
Medieval Italian vernacular

TIME AND PLACE WRITTEN
Early fourteenth century (probably begun around 1308 and
completed around 1314), throughout Italy

DATE OF FIRST PUBLICATION
1314

NARRATOR
The character Dante recounts his trip through Hell, looking
back on it after an indeterminate period of time.

POINT OF VIEW
As *Inferno* is an account of his own experiences, the character
Dante speaks in the first person from a subjective point of view,
giving the reader insight into his emotions and motivations.

TONE
Dante uses a largely moralistic tone when portraying the
figures and events in his poem. At times he also comes across as
sardonic or ironic. With his elaborately designed retributions,
Dante expresses a belief in, and awe for, the perfection of divine
justice.

TENSE
Past

SETTING (TIME)
The evening of Good Friday through the morning of Easter Sunday in the year 1300

SETTING (PLACE)
Hell

PROTAGONIST
On a literal level, Dante, the character in the poem; on an allegorical level, humankind

MAJOR CONFLICT
Dante attempts to find God in his life, while those sentenced to punishment in Hell hinder him from the true path.

CLIMAX
*Inferno* constitutes only the first third of a much larger work, *The Divine Comedy;* for this reason, and because of its extremely steady linear plot, *Inferno* has no real climax. The most dramatically significant moment in the poem probably arises in Dante's encounter with Lucifer, in Canto XXXIV, a scene that has struck generations of readers and critics as (deliberately) anticlimactic.

THEMES
The perfection of God's justice; evil as the contradiction of God's will; storytelling as a vehicle for immortality

MOTIFS
Political arguments; allusions to classical literature and mythology; cities; the role of fame and prestige in human life

SYMBOLS
*Inferno* is an allegory; nearly every element symbolizes some aspect of the theme. Most notably, the punishments of the sinners correspond symbolically to the sins themselves.

FORESHADOWING
Virgil occasionally makes references to events that occur later in the poem, and the Italian characters often prophesy Dante's exile from Florence, but, on the whole, *Inferno* contains little foreshadowing. Count Ugolino's gnawing on the head of the archbishop in Canto XXXIII may foreshadow Lucifer's gnawing on Brutus, Cassius, and Judas.

# STUDY QUESTIONS

1. *Describe the narrative form of* INFERNO. *How is it tied to the poem's geographical structure? How is it tied to the poem's central theme?*

The narrative of *Inferno* is extremely linear and progressive; the actions unfold over a sequence of increasingly extreme scenarios. Unlike most works of fiction, in which action is driven by the complex traits and motivations of characters, *Inferno* concerns itself very little with the personal qualities of Dante and Virgil. Rather, the narrative structure of the poem is directly tied to its geographical structure; the changing settings of the novel enable its sequence of encounters.

In a sense, the narrative structure of *Inferno* is based on the idea of the *degree* of sin found among the damned: Dante and Virgil move forward from the realm of the least offensive sinners to the realm of the most offensive sinners, so that they find themselves surrounded by a continuously increasing degree of evil and danger. By the same token, the geographical structure of the poem is based on the idea of the *kind* of sin committed by the damned; each new circle of Hell is designed specifically to punish a certain kind of sinner. Because of the allegorical correspondence between the type of sin and the type of punishment, the type of sin determines a great deal about the physical environment in which each scenario takes place. This cohesion between geography and story, and between type of sin and degree of sin, links the poem thematically to the idea of divine retribution and God's justice.

2. *Think about the role of character, apart from setting and story, in* INFERNO. *Does the poem contain any character development?*

*Inferno* contains very little character development. The narrative is driven by the two main characters' physical movement rather than psychological dynamics. Most characters appear in a particular canto, tell their story to Dante, and then disappear from the poem, as befits its episodic structure. In fact, one of the themes of Dante's exploration of the afterlife is that the dead are doomed to retain all of the features that they possessed on Earth, making character development difficult or perhaps even impossible for the poem's many shades.

Dante is the only character in the poem who can be said to develop. Virgil exhibits new behaviors from time to time, as when he castigates Dante in Canto XXX, but, in these moments, we sense that Virgil himself has not changed as a result of his experiences; rather, it seems that we see new sides of him as he enters new situations. Dante's development essentially follows a linear progression: he goes from pitying the damned souls to passing cold judgment on them. This change of behavior may correspond to a moral and intellectual realization that sin should be unreservedly abhorred and God's justice infinitely revered.

However, one may still question whether Dante's changes in behavior and apparent attitude actually correspond to any true development. First, he periodically seems to regress and regain his old compassion. Second, some of the disgust with which he views sinners in the final cantos can surely be attributed to the increasing vileness of their sins and punishments rather than to a growing moral consciousness.

3. *What is the role of politics in* INFERNO? *How does it relate to the poem's theme of divine justice?*

Throughout the poem, Dante the character repeatedly meets damned Italian souls with whom he then discusses events in Italy. These encounters give Dante the poet a chance to insert many political opinions, some of which relate to the poem's main moral and religious themes. Dante took politics very seriously, and his incorporation of so much political material into his journey through Hell serves the double purpose of situating his own political ideals in a larger moral scheme and warning his readers about the dangers of his enemies' political ideals.

By the end of the poem, Dante manages to unite his main political theme with his main religious theme in a figurative manner—by showing Lucifer chewing on Judas (the betrayer of Christ) and also on Cassius and Brutus (the betrayers of Julius Caesar). If Christ is taken to represent the perfect spiritual leader and Caesar the perfect temporal leader, then the inclusion of their betrayers among the worst sinners in Hell underscores Dante's politicized idea that church and state should be of equal importance in earthly governance. As Dante intended his work to ruminate more centrally on spiritual matters than on political ones, his discussion of human government in his religious allegory may constitute a plea for an earthly justice that might mirror the perfect justice of the afterlife.

# How to Write
# Literary Analysis

## The Literary Essay: A Step-by-Step Guide

When you read for pleasure, your only goal is enjoyment. You might find yourself reading to get caught up in an exciting story, to learn about an interesting time or place, or just to pass time. Maybe you're looking for inspiration, guidance, or a reflection of your own life. There are as many different, valid ways of reading a book as there are books in the world.

When you read a work of literature in an English class, however, you're being asked to read in a special way: you're being asked to perform *literary analysis*. To analyze something means to break it down into smaller parts and then examine how those parts work, both individually and together. Literary analysis involves examining all the parts of a novel, play, short story, or poem—elements such as character, setting, tone, and imagery—and thinking about how the author uses those elements to create certain effects.

A literary essay isn't a book review: you're not being asked whether or not you liked a book or whether you'd recommend it to another reader. A literary essay also isn't like the kind of book report you wrote when you were younger, where your teacher wanted you to summarize the book's action. A high school- or college-level literary essay asks, "How does this piece of literature actually work?" "How does it do what it does?" and, "Why might the author have made the choices he or she did?"

### The Seven Steps
No one is born knowing how to analyze literature; it's a skill you learn and a process you can master. As you gain more practice with this kind of thinking and writing, you'll be able to craft a method that works best for you. But until then, here are seven basic steps to writing a well-constructed literary essay:

1. *Ask questions*
2. *Collect evidence*
3. *Construct a thesis*

*4. Develop and organize arguments*
*5. Write the introduction*
*6. Write the body paragraphs*
*7. Write the conclusion*

## 1. ASK QUESTIONS

When you're assigned a literary essay in class, your teacher will often provide you with a list of writing prompts. Lucky you! Now all you have to do is choose one. Do yourself a favor and pick a topic that interests you. You'll have a much better (not to mention easier) time if you start off with something you enjoy thinking about. If you are asked to come up with a topic by yourself, though, you might start to feel a little panicked. Maybe you have too many ideas—or none at all. Don't worry. Take a deep breath and start by asking yourself these questions:

- **What struck you?** Did a particular image, line, or scene linger in your mind for a long time? If it fascinated you, chances are you can draw on it to write a fascinating essay.

- **What confused you?** Maybe you were surprised to see a character act in a certain way, or maybe you didn't understand why the book ended the way it did. Confusing moments in a work of literature are like a loose thread in a sweater: if you pull on it, you can unravel the entire thing. Ask yourself why the author chose to write about that character or scene the way he or she did and you might tap into some important insights about the work as a whole.

- **Did you notice any patterns?** Is there a phrase that the main character uses constantly or an image that repeats throughout the book? If you can figure out how that pattern weaves through the work and what the significance of that pattern is, you've almost got your entire essay mapped out.

- **Did you notice any contradictions or ironies?** Great works of literature are complex; great literary essays recognize and explain those complexities. Maybe the title (*Happy Days*) totally disagrees with the book's subject matter (hungry orphans dying in the woods). Maybe the main character acts one way around his family and a completely different way around his friends and associates. If you can find a way to explain a work's contradictory elements, you've got the seeds of a great essay.

At this point, you don't need to know exactly what you're going to say about your topic; you just need a place to begin your exploration. You can help direct your reading and brainstorming by formulating your topic as a *question,* which you'll then try to answer in your essay. The best questions invite critical debates and discussions, not just a rehashing of the summary. Remember, you're looking for something you can *prove or argue* based on evidence you find in the text. Finally, remember to keep the scope of your question in mind: is this a topic you can adequately address within the word or page limit you've been given? Conversely, is this a topic big enough to fill the required length?

## Good Questions

*"Are Romeo and Juliet's parents responsible for the deaths of their children?"*

*"Why do pigs keep showing up in* Lord of the Flies*?"*

*"Are Dr. Frankenstein and his monster alike? How?"*

## Bad Questions

*"What happens to Scout in* To Kill a Mockingbird*?"*

*"What do the other characters in* Julius Caesar *think about Caesar?"*

*"How does Hester Prynne in* The Scarlet Letter *remind me of my sister?"*

---

## 2. Collect Evidence

Once you know what question you want to answer, it's time to scour the book for things that will help you answer the question. Don't worry if you don't know what you want to say yet—right now you're just collecting ideas and material and letting it all percolate. Keep track of passages, symbols, images, or scenes that deal with your topic. Eventually, you'll start making connections between these examples and your thesis will emerge.

Here's a brief summary of the various parts that compose each and every work of literature. These are the elements that you will analyze in your essay, and which you will offer as evidence to support your arguments. For more on the parts of literary works, see the Glossary of Literary Terms at the end of this section.

LITERARY ANALYSIS

ELEMENTS OF STORY  These are the *what*s of the work—what happens, where it happens, and to whom it happens.

- **Plot:** All of the events and actions of the work.

- **Character:** The people who act and are acted upon in a literary work. The main character of a work is known as the *protagonist*.

- **Conflict:** The central tension in the work. In most cases, the protagonist wants something, while opposing forces (antagonists) hinder the protagonist's progress.

- **Setting:** When and where the work takes place. Elements of setting include location, time period, time of day, weather, social atmosphere, and economic conditions.

- **Narrator:** The person telling the story. The narrator may straightforwardly report what happens, convey the subjective opinions and perceptions of one or more characters, or provide commentary and opinion in his or her own voice.

- **Themes:** The main idea or message of the work—usually an abstract idea about people, society, or life in general. A work may have many themes, which may be in tension with one another.

ELEMENTS OF STYLE  These are the *how*s—how the characters speak, how the story is constructed, and how language is used throughout the work.

- **Structure and organization:** How the parts of the work are assembled. Some novels are narrated in a linear, chronological fashion, while others skip around in time. Some plays follow a traditional three- or five-act structure, while others are a series of loosely connected scenes. Some authors deliberately leave gaps in their works, leaving readers to puzzle out the missing information. A work's structure and organization can tell you a lot about the kind of message it wants to convey.

- **Point of view:** The perspective from which a story is told. In *first-person point of view,* the narrator involves him or herself in the story. ("I went to the store"; "We watched in horror as the bird slammed into the window.") A first-person narrator is usually the protagonist of the work, but not always. In *third-person point of view,* the narrator does not participate in the story. A third-person narrator may closely follow a specific character, recounting that individual character's thoughts or experiences, or it may be what we call an *omniscient* narrator. Omniscient narrators see and know all: they can witness any event in any time or place and are privy to the inner thoughts and feelings of all characters. Remember that the narrator and the author are not the same thing!

- **Diction:** Word choice. Whether a character uses dry, clinical language or flowery prose with lots of exclamation points can tell you a lot about his or her attitude and personality.

- **Syntax:** Word order and sentence construction. Syntax is a crucial part of establishing an author's narrative voice. Ernest Hemingway, for example, is known for writing in very short, straightforward sentences, while James Joyce characteristically wrote in long, incredibly complicated lines.

- **Tone:** The mood or feeling of the text. Diction and syntax often contribute to the tone of a work. A novel written in short, clipped sentences that use small, simple words might feel brusque, cold, or matter-of-fact.

- **Imagery:** Language that appeals to the senses, representing things that can be seen, smelled, heard, tasted, or touched.

- **Figurative language:** Language that is not meant to be interpreted literally. The most common types of figurative language are *metaphors* and *similes,* which compare two unlike things in order to suggest a similarity between them— for example, "All the world's a stage," or "The moon is like a ball of green cheese." (Metaphors say one thing *is* another thing; similes claim that one thing is *like* another thing.)

---

3. CONSTRUCT A THESIS

When you've examined all the evidence you've collected and know how you want to answer the question, it's time to write your thesis statement. A *thesis* is a claim about a work of literature that needs to be supported by evidence and arguments. The thesis statement is the heart of the literary essay, and the bulk of your paper will be spent trying to prove this claim. A good thesis will be:

- **Arguable.** "*The Great Gatsby* describes New York society in the 1920s" isn't a thesis—it's a fact.

- **Provable through textual evidence**. "*Hamlet* is a confusing but ultimately very well-written play" is a weak thesis because it offers the writer's personal opinion about the book. Yes, it's arguable, but it's not a claim that can be proved or supported with examples taken from the play itself.

- **Surprising**. "Both George and Lenny change a great deal in *Of Mice and Men*" is a weak thesis because it's obvious. A really strong thesis will argue for a reading of the text that is not immediately apparent.

- **Specific**. "Dr. Frankenstein's monster tells us a lot about the human condition" is *almost* a really great thesis statement, but it's still too vague. What does the writer mean by "a lot"? *How* does the monster tell us so much about the human condition?

## Good Thesis Statements

**Question:** In *Romeo and Juliet*, which is more powerful in shaping the lovers' story: fate or foolishness?

**Thesis:** "Though Shakespeare defines Romeo and Juliet as 'star-crossed lovers' and images of stars and planets appear throughout the play, a closer examination of that celestial imagery reveals that the stars are merely witnesses to the characters' foolish activities and not the causes themselves."

**Question:** How does the bell jar function as a symbol in Sylvia Plath's *The Bell Jar*?

**Thesis:** "A bell jar is a bell-shaped glass that has three basic uses: to hold a specimen for observation, to contain gases, and to maintain a vacuum. The bell jar appears in each of these capacities in *The Bell Jar*, Plath's semi-autobiographical novel, and each appearance marks a different stage in Esther's mental breakdown."

**Question:** Would Piggy in *The Lord of the Flies* make a good island leader if he were given the chance?

**Thesis:** "Though the intelligent, rational, and innovative Piggy has the mental characteristics of a good leader, he ultimately lacks the social skills necessary to be an effective one. Golding emphasizes this point by giving Piggy a foil in the charismatic Jack, whose magnetic personality allows him to capture and wield power effectively, if not always wisely."

---

## 4. DEVELOP AND ORGANIZE ARGUMENTS

The reasons and examples that support your thesis will form the middle paragraphs of your essay. Since you can't really write your thesis statement until you know how you'll structure your argument, you'll probably end up working on steps 3 and 4 at the same time.

There's no single method of argumentation that will work in every context. One essay prompt might ask you to compare and contrast two characters, while another asks you to trace an image through a given work of literature. These questions require different kinds of answers and therefore different kinds of arguments. Below, we'll discuss three common kinds of essay prompts and some strategies for constructing a solid, well-argued case.

### TYPES OF LITERARY ESSAYS

- **Compare and contrast**

  *Compare and contrast the characters of Huck and Jim in* THE ADVENTURES OF HUCKLEBERRY FINN.

  Chances are you've written this kind of essay before. In an academic literary context, you'll organize your arguments the same way you would in any other class. You can either go *subject by subject* or *point by point*. In the former, you'll discuss one character first and then the second. In the latter, you'll choose several traits (attitude toward life, social status, images and metaphors associated with the character) and devote a paragraph to each. You may want to use a mix of these two approaches—for example, you may want to spend a paragraph a piece broadly sketching Huck's and Jim's personalities before transitioning into a paragraph or two that describes a few key points of comparison. This can be a highly effective strategy if you want to make a counterintuitive argument—that, despite seeming to be totally different, the two objects being compared are actually similar in a very important way (or vice versa). Remember that your essay should reveal something fresh or unexpected about the text, so think beyond the obvious parallels and differences.

- **Trace**

  *Choose an image—for example, birds, knives, or eyes—and trace that image throughout* MACBETH.

  Sounds pretty easy, right? All you need to do is read the play, underline every appearance of a knife in *Macbeth*, and then list them in your essay in the order they appear, right? Well, not exactly. Your teacher doesn't want a simple catalog of examples. He or she wants to see you make *connections* between those examples—that's the difference between summarizing and analyzing. In the *Macbeth* example above, think about the different contexts in which knives appear in the play and to what effect. In *Macbeth*, there are real knives and imagined knives; knives that kill and knives that simply threaten. Categorize and classify your examples to give them some order. Finally, always keep the overall effect in mind. After you choose and analyze your examples, you should come to some greater understanding about the work, as well as your chosen image, symbol, or phrase's role in developing the major themes and stylistic strategies of that work.

- **Debate**

   *Is the society depicted in 1984 good for its citizens?*

   In this kind of essay, you're being asked to debate a moral, ethical, or aesthetic issue regarding the work. You might be asked to judge a character or group of characters (*Is Caesar responsible for his own demise?*) or the work itself (*Is JANE EYRE a feminist novel?*). For this kind of essay, there are two important points to keep in mind. First, don't simply base your arguments on your personal feelings and reactions. Every literary essay expects you to read and analyze the work, so search for evidence in the text. What do characters in *1984* have to say about the government of Oceania? What images does Orwell use that might give you a hint about his attitude toward the government? As in any debate, you also need to make sure that you define all the necessary terms before you begin to argue your case. What does it mean to be a "good" society? What makes a novel "feminist"? You should define your terms right up front, in the first paragraph after your introduction.

   Second, remember that strong literary essays make contrary and surprising arguments. Try to think outside the box. In the *1984* example above, it seems like the obvious answer would be no, the totalitarian society depicted in Orwell's novel is *not* good for its citizens. But can you think of any arguments for the opposite side? Even if your final assertion is that the novel depicts a cruel, repressive, and therefore harmful society, acknowledging and responding to the counterargument will strengthen your overall case.

## 5. WRITE THE INTRODUCTION

Your introduction sets up the entire essay. It's where you present your topic and articulate the particular issues and questions you'll be addressing. It's also where you, as the writer, introduce yourself to your readers. A persuasive literary essay immediately establishes its writer as a knowledgeable, authoritative figure.

An introduction can vary in length depending on the overall length of the essay, but in a traditional five-paragraph essay it should be no longer than one paragraph. However long it is, your introduction needs to:

- **Provide any necessary context.** Your introduction should situate the reader and let him or her know what to expect. What book are you discussing? Which characters? What topic will you be addressing?

- **Answer the "So what?" question.** Why is this topic important, and why is your particular position on the topic noteworthy? Ideally, your introduction should pique the reader's interest by suggesting how your argument is surprising or otherwise counterintuitive. Literary essays make unexpected connections and reveal less-than-obvious truths.

- **Present your thesis.** This usually happens at or very near the end of your introduction.

- **Indicate the shape of the essay to come.** Your reader should finish reading your introduction with a good sense of the scope of your essay as well as the path you'll take toward proving your thesis. You don't need to spell out every step, but you do need to suggest the organizational pattern you'll be using.

Your introduction should not:

- **Be vague.** Beware of the two killer words in literary analysis: *interesting* and *important*. Of course the work, question, or example is interesting and important—that's why you're writing about it!

- **Open with any grandiose assertions.** Many student readers think that beginning their essays with a flamboyant statement such as, "Since the dawn of time, writers have been fascinated with the topic of free will," makes them sound important and commanding. You know what? It actually sounds pretty amateurish.

- **Wildly praise the work.** Another typical mistake student writers make is extolling the work or author. Your teacher doesn't need to be told that "Shakespeare is perhaps the greatest writer in the English language." You can mention a work's reputation in passing—by referring to *The Adventures of Huckleberry Finn* as "Mark Twain's enduring classic," for example—but don't make a point of bringing it up unless that reputation is key to your argument.

- **Go off-topic.** Keep your introduction streamlined and to the point. Don't feel the need to throw in all kinds of bells and whistles in order to impress your reader—just get to the point as quickly as you can, without skimping on any of the required steps.

---

### 6. WRITE THE BODY PARAGRAPHS

Once you've written your introduction, you'll take the arguments you developed in step 4 and turn them into your body paragraphs. The organization of this middle section of your essay will largely be determined by the argumentative strategy you use, but no matter how you arrange your thoughts, your body paragraphs need to do the following:

- **Begin with a strong topic sentence.** Topic sentences are like signs on a highway: they tell the reader where they are and where they're going. A good topic sentence not only alerts readers to what issue will be discussed in the following paragraph but also gives them a sense of what argument will be made *about* that issue. "Rumor and gossip play an important role in *The Crucible*" isn't a strong topic sentence because it doesn't tell us very much. "The community's constant gossiping creates an environment that allows false accusations to flourish" is a much stronger topic sentence— it not only tells us *what* the paragraph will discuss (gossip) but *how* the paragraph will discuss the topic (by showing how gossip creates a set of conditions that leads to the play's climactic action).

- **Fully and completely develop a single thought.** Don't skip around in your paragraph or try to stuff in too much material. Body paragraphs are like bricks: each individual one needs to be strong and sturdy or the entire structure will collapse. Make sure you have really proven your point before moving on to the next one.

- **Use transitions effectively.** Good literary essay writers know that each paragraph must be clearly and strongly linked to the material around it. Think of each paragraph as a response to the one that precedes it. Use transition words and phrases such as *however, similarly, on the contrary, therefore,* and *furthermore* to indicate what kind of response you're making.

---

### 7. Write the Conclusion

Just as you used the introduction to ground your readers in the topic before providing your thesis, you'll use the conclusion to quickly summarize the specifics learned thus far and then hint at the broader implications of your topic. A good conclusion will:

- **Do more than simply restate the thesis.** If your thesis argued that *The Catcher in the Rye* can be read as a Christian allegory, don't simply end your essay by saying, "And that is why *The Catcher in the Rye* can be read as a Christian allegory." If you've constructed your arguments well, this kind of statement will just be redundant.

- **Synthesize the arguments, not summarize them.** Similarly, don't repeat the details of your body paragraphs in your conclusion. The reader has already read your essay, and chances are it's not so long that they've forgotten all your points by now.

- **Revisit the "So what?" question.** In your introduction, you made a case for why your topic and position are important. You should close your essay with the same sort of gesture. What do your readers know now that they didn't know before? How will that knowledge help them better appreciate or understand the work overall?

- **Move from the specific to the general.** Your essay has most likely treated a very specific element of the work—a single character, a small set of images, or a particular passage. In your conclusion, try to show how this narrow discussion has wider implications for the work overall. If your essay on *To Kill a Mockingbird* focused on the character of Boo Radley, for example, you might want to include a bit in your conclusion about how he fits into the novel's larger message about childhood, innocence, or family life.

- **Stay relevant.** Your conclusion should suggest new directions of thought, but it shouldn't be treated as an opportunity to pad your essay with all the extra, interesting ideas you came up with during your brainstorming sessions but couldn't fit into the essay proper. Don't attempt to stuff in unrelated queries or too many abstract thoughts.

- **Avoid making overblown closing statements.** A conclusion should open up your highly specific, focused discussion, but it should do so without drawing a sweeping lesson about life or human nature. Making such observations may be part of the point of reading, but it's almost always a mistake in essays, where these observations tend to sound overly dramatic or simply silly.

---

## A+ ESSAY CHECKLIST

Congratulations! If you've followed all the steps we've outlined above, you should have a solid literary essay to show for all your efforts. What if you've got your sights set on an A+? To write the kind of superlative essay that will be rewarded with a perfect grade, keep the following rubric in mind. These are the qualities that teachers expect to see in a truly A+ essay. How does yours stack up?

- ✓ Demonstrates a thorough understanding of the book
- ✓ Presents an original, compelling argument
- ✓ Thoughtfully analyzes the text's formal elements
- ✓ Uses appropriate and insightful examples
- ✓ Structures ideas in a logical and progressive order
- ✓ Demonstrates a mastery of sentence construction, transitions, grammar, spelling, and word choice

# SUGGESTED ESSAY TOPICS

1. *In what way is* INFERNO *a work of imagination and art rather than one of religion and philosophy alone? How do the poem's fantastic, imaginative, and dramatic elements contribute to its overall effectiveness?*

2. *What role does Aristotle's philosophy play in the moral scheme of* INFERNO? *How does it affect the poem's treatment of religious doctrine and Scripture?*

3. *What are some of the styles that Dante uses in* INFERNO? *What are some of the literary traditions to which the poem belongs? How does Dante's stylistic diversity affect his larger presentation of Hell?*

4. *How does allegory function in* INFERNO? *Think about the subject on both a universal level (*INFERNO *as an Everyman story) and a particular level (the correspondence between specific punishments and specific sins).*

# A+ Student Essay

What attitudes toward Christianity does Dante express in *Inferno*?

Dante's *Inferno* is an undeniably Christian text, as it catalogs various types of earthly sinners and describes the torments they experience in hell. The poem is the first part of Dante's three-part religious project, the *Divine Comedy,* which goes on to illustrate Christian purgatory and heaven. The *Inferno,* however, is much more than a mere dramatization of the Christian afterlife. In fact, while Dante exalts Christianity, he uses the *Inferno* to criticize the Church and its leaders, drawing a clear distinction between the faith and the institution—the former being holy and inviolate, the latter being fallible and corruptible.

Throughout the *Inferno,* Dante expresses his strict belief that Christianity is the one true religion. Admission to heaven, purgatory, and usually even hell is predicated on one's belief in Jesus' divinity. Ignorance of Jesus' existence, Dante asserts, is no excuse for non-belief. Good people born before the coming of Christ, such as Aristotle, Plato, and even Virgil himself, are condemned to an eternal state of limbo in the first circle of hell. Not even Moses or Noah, faithful men of the Old Testament, could leave limbo for heaven until Jesus had given them permission to do so. Dante's belief that nonbelievers exist in a transient state of incompletion in the afterlife suggests that he believes their lives were also deficient in the mortal world; otherwise, they would have ascended to heaven or even purgatory after death. To Dante, Christianity is therefore not only the key to salvation, but also integral to his understanding of what it means to be a good, whole person.

Despite his commitment to Christianity as the only true faith, however, Dante consigns a high number of church officials to hell. With few exceptions, every sinner Dante meets after leaving limbo had believed in Christ while alive, or at least been baptized. And yet, as Dante stresses throughout the *Inferno,* not even extreme faith or a clergy position can protect a true sinner from damnation. As Dante descends deeper into hell, Virgil repeatedly points out high-ranking church officials, including the traitorous Pope Anastasius in the seventh circle and the Archbishop Ruggieri in the second ring of the ninth circle. In the fourth circle, where the prodigal and avaricious must spend eternity pulling stone weights, Virgil and Dante encounter a throng of corrupt priests, cardinals, and popes too numerous to count or even recognize. By placing church officials in hell, Dante draws a distinction between the Christian faith and the institution of the Christian church, asserting that participation in the latter does not necessarily imply possession of the former.

Dante's simultaneous commitment to a strict Christianity and his condemnation of clergymen reflects his deeply held concerns about the institution of the Church. Dante's greatest ire is reserved for church leaders who drift from their ecclesiastical responsibilities—providing spiritual guidance to the people—in favor of chasing money and power. In the third pouch of the eighth circle of hell, for example, Dante encounters the Simoniacs, church leaders who have sold ecclesiastical offices for money and personal gain. In Canto XIX, he meets Pope Nicholas III, who must spend the rest of eternity upside down, his head in a rock and his feet (which have been set aflame) in the air, for having abused his spiritual authority to increase the political power of the Church. The sight provokes Dante to launch an invective against papal abuses of power, crying out against the "miserable lot" of clergymen who "take the things of God that ought to be / Wedded to goodness and in your greediness / Adulterate them into gold and silver!" As he progresses through the *Inferno,* it becomes clear that, in Dante's eyes, the Church has become so corrupt that it has lost its spiritual authority, severing the link between the faith and the institution.

Though the *Inferno* purports to treat eternal truths about sin and punishment, its depiction of hell is rooted in the political realities of Dante's particular time and place. As a member of a Florentine political party known as the White Guelphs, Dante advocated the separation of church and state, which eventually led to his banishment from Florence in 1302. In Canto XIX, he decries the fusion of politics and spirituality, blaming the Roman emperor Constantine for the "foul harm [he] fostered" when he converted to Christianity and gave control of Rome to "the first wealthy father," the pope. Dante believed that giving the Church political power distracted the clergy from their spiritual duties, corrupting them in the process. He agitated for change in real life, and with the *Inferno,* he subtly suggests that the Church should abandon its quest for secular power in order to reclaim its spiritual authority over the Christian faith and its itinerants.

# GLOSSARY OF LITERARY TERMS

ANTAGONIST

The entity that acts to frustrate the goals of the *protagonist*. The antagonist is usually another *character* but may also be a non-human force.

ANTIHERO / ANTIHEROINE

A *protagonist* who is not admirable or who challenges notions of what should be considered admirable.

CHARACTER

A person, animal, or any other thing with a personality that appears in a *narrative*.

CLIMAX

The moment of greatest intensity in a text or the major turning point in the *plot*.

CONFLICT

The central struggle that moves the *plot* forward. The conflict can be the *protagonist*'s struggle against fate, nature, society, or another person.

FIRST-PERSON POINT OF VIEW

A literary style in which the *narrator* tells the story from his or her own *point of view* and refers to himself or herself as "I." The narrator may be an active participant in the story or just an observer.

HERO / HEROINE

The principal *character* in a literary work or *narrative*.

IMAGERY

Language that brings to mind sense-impressions, representing things that can be seen, smelled, heard, tasted, or touched.

MOTIF

A recurring idea, structure, contrast, or device that develops or informs the major *themes* of a work of literature.

NARRATIVE

A story.

NARRATOR

The person (sometimes a *character*) who tells a story; the *voice* assumed by the writer. The narrator and the author of the work of literature are not the same person.

PLOT

The arrangement of the events in a story, including the sequence in which they are told, the relative emphasis they are given, and the causal connections between events.

POINT OF VIEW

The *perspective* that a *narrative* takes toward the events it describes.

PROTAGONIST

The main *character* around whom the story revolves.

SETTING

The location of a *narrative* in time and space. Setting creates mood or atmosphere.

SUBPLOT

A secondary *plot* that is of less importance to the overall story but may serve as a point of contrast or comparison to the main plot.

SYMBOL

An object, *character,* figure, or color that is used to represent an abstract idea or concept. Unlike an *emblem,* a symbol may have different meanings in different contexts.

SYNTAX

The way the words in a piece of writing are put together to form lines, phrases, or clauses; the basic structure of a piece of writing.

THEME

A fundamental and universal idea explored in a literary work.

TONE

The author's attitude toward the subject or *characters* of a story or poem or toward the reader.

VOICE

An author's individual way of using language to reflect his or her own personality and attitudes. An author communicates voice through *tone, diction,* and *syntax.*

LITERARY ANALYSIS

# A Note on Plagiarism

Plagiarism—presenting someone else's work as your own—rears its ugly head in many forms. Many students know that copying text without citing it is unacceptable. But some don't realize that even if you're not quoting directly, but instead are paraphrasing or summarizing, *it is plagiarism* unless you cite the source.

Here are the most common forms of plagiarism:

- Using an author's phrases, sentences, or paragraphs without citing the source
- Paraphrasing an author's ideas without citing the source
- Passing off another student's work as your own

How do you steer clear of plagiarism? You should *always* acknowledge all words and ideas that aren't your own by using quotation marks around verbatim text or citations like footnotes and endnotes to note another writer's ideas. For more information on how to give credit when credit is due, ask your teacher for guidance or visit www.sparknotes.com.

# REVIEW & RESOURCES

## QUIZ

1. On what Christian holy day does *Inferno* begin?

    A. Good Friday
    B. Christmas
    C. The Feast of All Saints
    D. Michaelmas

2. How old is Dante at the beginning of the poem?

    A. 45
    B. 40
    C. 35
    D. 31

3. What human quality is Virgil usually thought to represent?

    A. Compassion
    B. Reason
    C. Justice
    D. Vehemence

4. Which group of sinners must remain submerged in the swampy Styx?

    A. The Uncommitted
    B. The Traitors to Their Kin
    C. The Heretics
    D. The Sullen

5. What is the meaning of the word "Malebranche"?

    A. Evil Claws
    B. Evil Eyes
    C. Evil Pockets
    D. Evil Deeds

6. Of which Florentine political party was Farinata a leader?

    A.  The Black Guelphs
    B.  The White Guelphs
    C.  The Social Democrats
    D.  The Ghibellines

7. Where does Beatrice reside after death?

    A.  Hell
    B.  Heaven
    C.  Purgatory
    D.  Nirvana

8. Why is Judas unable to speak?

    A.  His tongue is a writhing snake.
    B.  His lips are made of fire.
    C.  His head lies frozen beneath the ice.
    D.  Lucifer is chewing on his head.

9. What event caused the earthquake mentioned by several demons and spirits in the poem?

    A.  Christ's death
    B.  God's defeat of Lucifer in the war of the angels
    C.  The rebellion of the Gluttonous 300 years earlier
    D.  The Evisceration of the Damned

10. Who tells Dante the story of Paolo and Francesca?

    A.  Paolo
    B.  Virgil
    C.  Francesca
    D.  Dido

11. A Centaur is a cross between which two creatures?

    A.  Woman and bird
    B.  Man and horse
    C.  Eagle and lion
    D.  Lion and scorpion

12. Which three beasts block Dante from the sunlit hill in Canto I?

    A. A lion, a stag, and a serpent
    B. A unicorn, a tiger, and a boar
    C. A boar-hound, a greyhound, and a mastiff
    D. A leopard, a lion, and a she-wolf

13. From which city was Dante exiled?

    A. Florence
    B. Mantua
    C. Naples
    D. Rome

14. Which pope was Dante's enemy?

    A. Innocent XVIII
    B. Clement I
    C. Boniface VIII
    D. Liberius

15. Into how many "pouches" is the Eighth Circle of Hell divided?

    A. Nine
    B. Ten
    C. Eleven
    D. Twelve

16. How many circles constitute Dante's Hell?

    A. Five
    B. Seven
    C. Eleven
    D. Nine

17. Which city did Dante believe to be more important than all others?

    A. Florence
    B. Rome
    C. Paris
    D. Alexandria

18. Who brings Dante from the Eighth to the Ninth Circle of Hell?

    A. Lucifer
    B. Virgil
    C. Antaeus
    D. A divine messenger

19. What words can be found above the Gate of Hell?

    A. ABANDON ALL HOPE, YOU WHO ENTER HERE
    B. AND JUSTICE FOR ALL
    C. IN THE NAME OF GOD, AMEN
    D. REMAINING FROGS

20. Who opens the gates of Dis?

    A. Virgil
    B. Dante
    C. Demons
    D. An angelic messenger

21. What is Geryon thought to represent?

    A. Pity
    B. Violence
    C. Joy
    D. Fraud

22. Which river must souls cross before they enter Hell?

    A. The Avillon
    B. The Acheron
    C. The Styx
    D. The Lethe

23. Where in Hell does Virgil reside?

    A. Malebolge
    B. The Styx
    C. Limbo
    D. The Ante-Inferno

24. Where do the Spenders and Hoarders receive their punishment?

    A.   In the Fourth Circle
    B.   In the Second Circle
    C.   In the Fifth Circle
    D.   In the Sixth Pouch of the Eighth Circle

25. What form of verse does *Inferno* utilize?

    A.   Sonnet
    B.   Alexandrine
    C.   Heroic couplet
    D.   Terza rima

ANSWER KEY

1: A; 2: C; 3: B; 4: D; 5: A; 6: D; 7: B; 8: D; 9: A; 10: C; 11: B; 12: D;
13: A; 14: C; 15: B; 16: D; 17: B; 18: C; 19: A; 20: D; 21: D; 22: B;
23: C; 24: A; 25: D

## SUGGESTIONS FOR FURTHER READING

ALIGHIERI, DANTE. *Paradiso*. Trans. John Ciardi. New York: New American Library, 1987.

———. *Purgatorio*. Trans. John Ciardi. New York: New American Library, 1987.

AUERBACH, ERICH. *Mimesis: The Representation of Reality in Western Literature*. Trans. Willard R. Trask. Princeton, NJ: Princeton University Press, 1953.

BLOOM, HAROLD, ed. *Dante's* THE DIVINE COMEDY: *Modern Critical Interpretations*. New York: Chelsea House Publishers, 1987.

CHIARENZA, MARGUERITE. THE DIVINE COMEDY: *Tracing God's Art*. Boston: Twayne Publishers, 1989.

HIMMELFARB, MARTHA. *Tours of Hell: An Apocalyptic Form in Jewish and Christian Literature*. Philadelphia: University of Pennsylvania Press, 1983.

TIERNEY, BRIAN, ed. *The Crisis of the Church & State: 1050–1300*. Englewood Cliffs, NJ: Prentice Hall, Inc., 1964.

REVIEW & RESOURCES

# SparkNotes Literature Guides

Visit sparknotes.com for many more!